£5

£c

D1580059

CHANCE AND
THE FIRE-HORSES

by the same author

RANGI, HIGHLAND RESCUE DOG

CHANCE AND THE FIRE-HORSES

Ernest Dudley

A Story that really happened,
taken from Log-Books, Official Documents
of the old London Fire Brigade, and
Old Firemen's remembrances

HARVILL PRESS

LONDON 1972

For their great help in bringing Chance and his
friends, the firemen and fire-horses, back to life,
grateful acknowledgements to: the Chief Officer
of the London Fire Brigade and his Staff, par-
ticularly Mr R. J. Wood, Historian; the late
George J. Murrell, Senior Superintendent; the
Librarians and Archivists; and to the staff of the
London Library.

© 1972 Ernest Dudley

ISBN 0 00 262102 9

Set in Monotype Caslon
Made and Printed in Great Britain by
William Collins Sons & Co Ltd Glasgow
for the Publishers Harvill Press Ltd
30A Pavilion Road, London SW1

Contents

Illustrations

Illustrations and Firemen's Verse extracts by permission of the Chief Officer of the London Fire Brigade and *The Illustrated London News*.

THE FIREMAN'S SONG

In the midwatch of the night,
   When the tongue of the booming bell
Sounds alarm, and flames burst on the sight,
   The Fire-King's deeds to tell,
A sound on the ear doth fall,
   That is borne on the heated blast,
'Tis the cheering note of the Fireman's call,
   As the engines rumble past.
The flames illume the sky,
   And, wrapt in a blazing wreath,
Our dear-loved homes are shown to the eye,
   As the revel place of Death.
And above the blasting gale,
   List to those piteous cries!
'Tis the sound of an infant's feeble wail,
   Amid blazing ruin dies.

But see! there's a rescue near,
   For from that countless mass,
While cheeks are bleached, hearts rent with fear,
   See the noble fireman pass!
He mounts the toppling stairs,
While the red flames fiercely dart,
And the child from the funeral pyre he bears
   To the shrine of its mother's heart.

God bless the firemen dear!
   A mother's widowed heart
Shall beat with joy and, the orphan's tear
   From the fount of love shall start.
And when the Fireman's death
   Shall call their fatal roll,
Their grateful prayers shall soar with his breath,
   And plead for the parting soul.

C. H. SAUNDERS

1. A Dog from Nowhere

'I'll do for that Braidwood!' then said he,
  'And the whole of the brigadier brood.
I'll make them respect my dignity,
  As every fireman should.
I'll set the Thames on fire, and see
  If he bilks me out of my food,'
Then away he tooled to Tooley Street,
  And selected a warehouse of oil.
         The Fire-Demon from *Town,*
         a contemporary magazine

At the dawn of the later stone age, there appears,
as the first domestic animal, a small semi-domesticated
dog.   KONRAD LORENZ

IT was a stock of hemp that caught fire in Scovell's warehouse on Cotton's Wharf which looked over Tooley Street at five o'clock, near as makes no matter, that Saturday afternoon, the 22nd of June 1861, and started off one of London's worst fires. Spontaneous combustion, it was said to have been. At any rate, the warehouse was stacked from floor to ceiling not only with hemp, but saltpetre, tallow, cotton, rice, sugar, tea and spices, and the whole place was soon ablaze. London's fire-brigade chief, James Braidwood – though destined to hold that post for only a few more hours - was on the scene with his fire-fighters within a few minutes of the alarm being raised.

Tooley Street backs on to the waterfront, and narrow

streets, more like alleys or lanes they were in those days, run from it to Cotton's Wharf and other warehouses on Hay's Wharf, Chamberlain's Wharf and the jetties off Pickle Herring Street as far as Tower Bridge. All filled from basement to roof with sulphur, tallow, chicory, flour, cheese, jute, oils and paint. The newly acquired fire-float, moored down at Southwark Bridge, was called in to pour water on to the inferno in an attempt to contain it. But without much avail. Ten thousand casks of melted tallow were soon flowing into the River Thames. Crowds on London Bridge saw men rowing out to salvage the tallow, admiration for their daring changing to horror as several of the rowboats, drawn by the tide's vortex into great patches of blazing tallow – the river itself seemed to have caught fire – caught alight and men burned to death.

At seven o'clock it was reported to Braidwood that the fire-float was working so close to the flames that the firemen's faces, hands and clothes were badly scorched, and how much longer would they be expected to continue? A man of deep religious convictions (he was concerned with helping London's ragged schools), quiet-voiced and possessed of a strong physique which could withstand exposure to the chill air on the one hand and the heat of the flames on the other, Braidwood never panicked, but reacted to any alarming emergency with cool decision. Queen Victoria had a soft spot in her heart for him: when on the 20th of March 1853, fire broke out in the Prince of Wales Tower at Windsor Castle, she had been unimpressed by the local firemen's efforts, and telegraphed Braidwood to bring his brigade by special train from London.

He had dealt with the situation with characteristic resourcefulness.

Now, he hurried along Tooley Street, to turn down one of the alleys to reach the river. He saw a fireman approaching, reeling from exhaustion. He made to move towards him to speak to him. At that moment a warehouse wall overlooking the alley suddenly collapsed, burying Braidwood in hot brickwork.

The news of his death caused consternation and despair among the sweating, smoke-blackened firemen. It seemed to them that their strenuous attempts to combat the spreading furnace were futile, the entire area of Tooley Street was doomed; but then the spirit of their dead chief seemed to assume command as before, and they found new strength to fight on. It was to be a fortnight before the fire was finally extinguished; it took three days to get it sufficiently under control so that Braidwood's charred body could be recovered from the smouldering ruins.

Queen Victoria sent a message of condolence to his widow; and despatched the Earl of Stamford to Tooley Street to learn the circumstances of his death and if his body had been found.

A curious thing had happened.

A dog, appearing from nowhere, led a fireman named Robert Tozer straight to the body; and then, Tozer recalled, had vanished. First it was there, then it wasn't. Other firemen, some who were older, said it was no dog, but a ghost – tales used to be told in the watch-room of spectral firemen, phantom horses, and ghostly dogs – more than likely, one fireman thought, the ghost of a dog named Chance. He was referring not to the dog Chance that this story is about, but another of the same name, who had appeared out of the blue years before, 1834 it would be, and raced the Watling Street fire-engine at every turn-out. He had died from injuries received in a fire. Could well be his ghost, the fireman said, that Tozer had seen, and followed to the body.

On the other hand, another fireman pointed out, old Chance, in between dashing off to fires, had managed to father a son and heir, but the pup had been stolen by a dog-thief and never seen again. Couldn't it have been a great-grandchild in whose veins ran its forbear's obsession with fire-fighting, who had turned up at Tooley Street? But others were more convinced that it was more likely to have been a ghost.

This gives you some notion of the strange yarns firemen used to tell, quoting numerous examples of 'the fascination', as one put it, 'of fire for the brute creation'. Such as Joe, whose collar is still preserved by the Oxford Fire Brigade, who accompanied the fire-engine to scores of fires, and carried messages back to the fire-station. He was credited with knowing the name of every volunteer fireman and would race un-erringly to their respective homes whenever reserve personnel were needed. Joe was a great barker, so much so that one member of the brigade, somewhat peeved by the noise, once described him as 'a bloody nuisance, forever barking his head off at the horses'.

Another dog, a Cockney mongrel named Tyke, attached himself to one London fire-brigade after another. 'His delight,' according to one fireman, 'is to be at all fires in the Metropolis; and far or near, we generally find him on the road as we go along. I do not think there has been a fire for eight or nine years which he has not attended.'

A Whitechapel dog, named Bob, though he sometimes became confused with the first Chance, followed a fireman to the East End Central Station, and although restored to his owner, refused to remain at home, escaping again and again. His legs had been broken half-a-dozen times, but he was back at the first fire he could find the moment he had recovered from his injuries. There was another Bob, of Holborn, who could run up a ladder, or jump through a window with more agility than any fireman. He saved a kitten at a fire in Duke Street, Manchester Square; a child at a Westminster Bridge Road fire; and met an untimely end under the hooves of fire-horses pelting to a blaze in Caledonian Road.

The famed adventure-novelist, R. M. Ballantyne, who for his book of fire tales drew on none other than the redoubtable fire-chief, Captain Shaw, described how in 1894 a Glasgow dog, named Wallace, became the local fire-fighters' mascot. Wallace's enthusiastic efforts to aid the firemen resulted in his suffering from chronically burned paws, so he had to be provided with a specially made pair of boots. A Salford dog, named Lion, became famous in the North for his heroism at nearly four hundred fires. He exhibited uncanny sagacity on one particular occasion, when a child was thought to have been left behind in a burning house. Lion duly dashed into the inferno, to reappear with the infant's cradle. Obviously he was endeavouring to convey that the late occupant must be elsewhere;

and as it transpired, the babe had been carried to safety by a neighbour.

There was also Nell, a retriever, at nearby Rochdale, who not only distinguished herself as a fire-fighter, but once saved a gentleman's hat from the river; refusing, however, to return it to its rightful owner, she insisted instead on taking it to the nearest police-station. Which, as Nell was fully aware, was the proper place for lost property.

A Liverpool dog, Carlo, was honoured with a special badge by the Liverpool Shipwreck and Humane Society for his display of bravery at a dock-side holocaust. Carlo marched with his proud owner, Fireman Cragg, at the Lord Mayor's 1885 Show in London, the *Daily Telegraph* reporting: 'The fireman's dog had the most notable reception of the day.' In the previous May, Bill, a terrier, attached to a Whitechapel fire-station for nine years – he'd been run over three times, could carry a guiding lantern dexterously between his teeth, and be up a ladder before any fireman had scaled it half-way – had received a special decoration for steadfast devotion to duty at a fire in Fashion Street, Spitalfields. Though falling into a tub of scalding water, which removed every hair on his body, he dashed to the aid of a fireman, named John Atkins, rendered semi-conscious, and dragged him from the flames.

What then was so strange about a dog which had been made so much of by the firemen, when it died, in a fire or from natural causes, returning as a ghost to the place it had known and loved? Well . . . you may believe in ghosts or not, of dogs or human beings, the fact remains that some twenty years after the Tooley Street fire, a stray mongrel did turn up out of nowhere, and became reckoned something of a hero in the annals of London's terrible fires.

This particular dog's story begins one Autumn evening in 1882, at Peckham, South London, where Thomas Tilling, the famous horse-master, had taken over the old Adam & Eve Stable Yard as a horse-omnibus station. Peckham was then virtually a village set in fields and market-gardens, and Tilling, who had horsed the local fire-station, the Surrey Volunteer Fire Brigade, was running a quarter-hourly bus-service to and from the City: 'A quarter arter, 'arf arter, quarter to, and at,' was the cryptic reply to the intending traveller inquiring about the time-table.

This dog who suddenly appeared on the scene was darkish brown, short-haired, a cross between a bull-terrier and a mastiff, you might say, with perhaps a few other breeds thrown in. A perpetually furrowed brow above shiny, popping eyes made you think that he must always have some question on his mind. A question to which you felt he knew instinctively he would never find the answer. If he knew for certain, that is, what exactly the question was.

Right from the start, he had chummed up with one of the bus-horses, named Bruce. Made straight for him while Bruce who had not long finished his day's work was being unharnessed, and singled him out from all the other horses. And Bruce took to him.

Every morning for the next six weeks, when Bruce went off to work, the dog would jump up at him, and bark, as if to say: look after yourself and I'll be here to welcome you when you come back. And he would be there, jumping up and barking at him to show how pleased he was to see Bruce again. He had an odd way of clicking his teeth when he was excited, which used to put the teeth of some of the bus-drivers and conductors on edge and send a cold shiver down their spines.

But everyone at Tilling's quickly grew fond of him; all noted how he had chummed up with Bruce, and how every night, half-an-hour before the bus-horse was due back from work the dog would start running about in a restless way, barking and click-clicking his teeth. He knew that his friend was on his way home, and he was ready to welcome him.

Then the dog disappeared. He had done the vanishing trick early one evening; rather the same way as when he'd arrived. One minute he was there, the next he was gone.

What had happened to him?

Where had he taken himself off to?

The same night, a newspaper-reporter named Jack While was hurrying to Fleet Street. His father was a *Times* reporter, and Jack following in his footsteps, had begun to specialise in reporting fires for *The Times* and also for other London newspapers. The *Pall Mall Gazette*, the *Globe*, the *Echo*, and the *Westminster Gazette*, all of which were eager for 'fire copy'. There wasn't much Jack While wasn't to come to learn about fires and the firemen who fought them. He had reached a quiet street leading to Fleet Street; it was quiet because the City was almost deserted at that time of night, the only place that was at all busy was Fleet

Street, where the next day's newspapers were being printed.

As he was passing some offices he noticed a light in a top window. He thought it was odd for anyone to be working in the offices at that late hour, but he didn't pay much attention to it as he was looking forward to an enjoyable meal at Evan's Supper Rooms, a famous eating-place in Covent Garden, to which his father had promised to take him. But as he hurried on he noticed that the light was flickering. Suddenly it seemed much brighter than a gas-lamp, or the light from a candle or an oil-lamp. Then he saw a tongue of flame shoot up and lick the window. He let out a yell: 'Fire . . . Fire . . . The place is on fire!'

His shouts brought a 'Charley', that's what a night-watchman was called, out of a nearby doorway, who took one look at the top floor, and dashed to the street-corner where there was a fire-post. It was the only sort of fire-alarm they had in London, then. The 'Charley' smashed the glass at the top of the post and pulled the handle.

*

The alarm rang in the watch-room of the nearest fire-station which was in Chandos Street, just by Charing Cross. A fireman named Dick Tozer, a son of that same Robert Tozer who nineteen years before had found Braidwood's body in Tooley Street, was on duty that night, and shouted to the other firemen. They buckled on belts and buttoned up uniforms while they clambered on *Fire Queen*, the fire-engine – officially described as a steamer, for the pump which drove the water by hose-pipe on to the flames was powered by steam. Tom Woods, nicknamed 'Coach', whose job was to drive and look after Bob and Betty, the horses, had already harnessed them up, and they were miraculously away in a matter of moments.

Along the Strand tore *Fire Queen*, sparks flying from Betty's and Bob's galloping hooves, the firemen shouting 'Hi-ya-hi' to clear the way. Alongside raced boys and young men, determined to see the fire. On, on, past the brightly-lit restaurants, the theatres, the Tivoli Music-Hall, sped Betty and Bob. Both were greys, Bob being much older than Betty, and loved by all the firemen. He was full of tricks: he would turn off the water-tap in the fire-engine yard with his teeth; he would playfully nip a fireman just as he bent down to pick up a length of hosepipe – all sorts of games old Bob enjoyed.

Suddenly, 'Coach' felt the engine pulling to one side. He looked at the horses. Old Bob was slowing down, and Betty was having to do his share of the work. 'Come on, Bob, pull your weight.' 'Coach' gave a gentle flick with the whip, Bob tossed his head and began to pull again, and *Fire Queen* straightened up. Past the Law Courts and into Fleet Street.

Sometimes, when Bob was in one of his lazy moods – increasingly of late, Tom Woods was realising, he felt like taking a bit of a rest – Betty would pull his weight for him. She was much gentler, affectionate, motherly almost, the way she would rub noses with Bob. She was very hard-working, always pulled with every ounce of her strength. And she would do Bob's work for him, and Tom Woods would have to shout at him, as he had tonight, to remind him he was supposed to do his share. 'Coach' had already spoken to Mr Goodwin, who was one of Tilling's horse-buyers, and mentioned that he was a bit worried about old Bob. The air was thick with smoke now. *Fire Queen* passed two newspaper offices then turned into a narrow street. There was the burning office-building, a great black cloud billowing from it, blotting out the stars in the sky. The crowd gave way as *Fire Queen* pulled up. 'Coach' unharnessed Bob and Betty and led them to a place further along, out of danger of crashing floor-beams, or collapsing walls. Dick Tozer and the other firemen were already connecting up to a water-hydrant, in no time at all the pump was sending streams of water on to the burning building. An escape-ladder had been brought, by which anyone trapped upstairs might be rescued.

A loud cheer rose from the crowd, and Jack While could be seen darting forward; he had his reporter's notebook ready, and scribbled in it with a pencil-stub. He had forgotten all about that supper with his father at Evan's, he was too caught up with this exciting slice of 'fire copy', anything else was completely driven out of his mind. In those days, when the telephone had barely come into use, and a reporter couldn't phone his story in, newspapers went to press much later than nowadays; Jack had plenty of time to gather information, even ride back with the fire-engine to head-quarters to check facts, write up a column or so, and dash off with it to Fleet Street in a hansom-cab, or send it by a messenger.

The cheering had been for a slim, trim, tall figure,

whom Jack recognised at once. The familiar, well-loved Captain Shaw, chief of London's fire-brigades who had arrived from his headquarters in Southwark on the other side of the river. He wore a long goatee beard, and his blue eyes were alert beneath his helmet, which was a special silver one; the other firemen wore helmets of brass. Captain Shaw was known as The Skipper, but usually nicknamed 'The Long 'Un' by his men.

At this moment Dick Tozer heard a shout from above. He looked up at the offices, but he could see nothing but smoke. The shout came again. He looked further to his left up at the office-building. Leaning out of a top floor window was a young man. Obviously some employee, a clerk no doubt, who had been working late. Now he was cut off by the fire which was spreading fast. Tongues of flame were already licking at the window-sill below him.

Captain Shaw gave an order, and Dick, together with another fireman, wheeled an escape-ladder over to the office-building. It was a heavy, cumbersome apparatus, a fifty-foot ladder on wheels, in sections which could be extended by pulling on the appropriate ropes. Dick and his companion quickly had the top section climbing upwards, higher and higher until it reached the top storey. Dick swarmed up. The young man was terrified, but Dick knew how to deal with him; he grabbed him smartly, slung him over his shoulder in what is called a fireman's lift, and carried him down to safety.

By now other fire-engines had raced up, and some two-score firemen were attacking the blaze. It looked as if it was going to be impossible to put it out before the whole building collapsed. More hose-pipes played the flames, still roaring higher, and black smoke billowed above. The ever-increasing crowd in the street wore anxious expressions, their faces reflecting the red malevolent fire. And the sooty dust fell everywhere.

Captain Shaw moved confidently among his men, directing the powerful streams of water on to the blaze, never asking for any job to be carried out he himself wouldn't, or couldn't, carry out; though he never shirked personal danger, he never ran an unnecessary risk, nor would he allow his men to do so. It was due to the ever-watchful supervision he kept over them when fighting a fire that accounted for their utter confidence in him. None ever hesitated to follow where he led.

It was then that the dog put in his appearance.

Suddenly, as if out of a magician's hat.

Now he wasn't there, then suddenly he was. Darkish brown, short-haired, a cross between a bull terrier and a mastiff, with perhaps a few other breeds added. Eyes very shiny, with a perpetually furrowed brow, as if he always had some question on his mind. He made straight for Dick Tozer who'd taken off his helmet and was mopping his blackened face with a handkerchief. The dog barked excitedly and jumped up at him.

'Hello, hello?' Dick was puzzled by his behaviour. 'What is it, then – ?' He rushed off to the open doorway of the building, from which Dick had rescued the clerk. The place was full of smoke, and beyond, scarlet and orange flames. He turned back to Dick, his eyes popping with excitement, then rushed back to the door. He wanted Dick to go in. No doubt about it. 'What is it? What's wrong?'

For answer the dog jumped up, grasped Dick's coat-sleeve and gave it a tug. He continued to try and calm him, but off he rushed to the open doorway again. 'If you could speak,' Dick said to him grimly, 'I know what you'd tell me. Someone's in there.'

Captain Shaw, who was standing near, saw the dog's excitement – you couldn't very well miss, the way he was carrying on – and realised what he was trying to communicate to Dick Tozer. Some of the crowd had surged forward, their attention on the dog. They sensed something dramatic, dangerous, was on the cards.

'Too risky,' the Skipper was saying. 'Ceiling might cave in . . .'

The dog was barking even more insistently as Dick pulled on his helmet and started for the door. He ran to and fro, his barks rising to a crescendo – then shot into the smoke-filled hallway. Dick glanced back at Captain Shaw.

'Someone is in there,' he shouted, and followed the dog.

There he was, scratching and barking at the door as if he would tear it down. He even leapt up at the door-handle in an attempt to turn it. Dick glanced up at the ceiling. It bulged, cracks zigzagged across it. He would have to risk it. He crossed to the door and turned the handle. It was jammed. He glanced at the dog, which seemed to understand and moved out of

The Tooley Street fire, 22nd June 1861. Braidwood died in a
street directly behind the blazing buildings

James Braidwood, Superintendent of
the London Fire Brigade

Plaque in Tooley Street to Braidwood's
memory: 'A just Man and one that
trusted God, and of good report among
all the Nation.'

'Fire!' Turn-out racing through the old Temple Bar

'Rescued!' London firemen at work

the way. Dick took a step back, then charged the door with his shoulder. It crashed down in a shower of sparks, and he stumbled over a young girl who lay just inside the room.

She had collapsed, overcome by the smoke. He picked her up, and rushed out into the street, the dog jumping up and barking – oh, he had known someone was in the room, all right. The crowd let out a cheer as Dick Tozer emerged with the girl in his arms; the fresh air revived her; she was opening her eyes. Muttering that she had remained late to finish her work, without anyone realising that she was there.

At this moment a deep, quiet voice with a slight foreign accent spoke into Dick Tozer's ear. 'Bravo . . . Bravo . . .'

Dick turned and stared into the face of the man beside him. At once he knew who he was. Short, pointed beard and plump features under his helmet – but it was a silver helmet which showed that he was no ordinary fireman, although he was wearing an ordinary fireman's uniform.

'Thank you, Your Royal Highness.'

It was the Prince of Wales. He was giving the dog a hearty pat, and his tail wagged energetically. It was not unusual for the Prince to attend a fire. He was a keen amateur fireman. Captain Shaw would telephone him at his home, Marlborough House in Pall Mall, opposite St James's Palace, to let him know if there was a fire raging. He would also send a carriage to collect him and bring him to Chandos Street Fire Station where his uniform and the silver helmet were kept in readiness for him.

Now he was explaining to Captain Shaw why he had arrived so late; he had been held up by the crowds which thronged Fleet Street and the street in which the office-building was blazing, and he had been compelled to get out of his carriage and continue on foot.

He set to with Dick Tozer and the rest of the firemen, working furiously. Meanwhile, the girl and the rescued young man were taken to their homes by a horse-drawn ambulance which was waiting on the outskirts of the crowd to look after victims of the fire.

As for the dog, he stayed close beside Dick, jumping in whenever he could to pull away smouldering pieces, undaunted by the hazard of flying sparks, or falling debris.

Presently, it looked as if the fire was under control, as if the firemen were winning. There was more steam in the air than smoke. The crowd was already beginning to drift away, gossiping among themselves about the fire and the rescue of the girl and the young man. And, of course, there was any amount of wonder and admiration for the dog.

The acrid smell of burning wood mingled with the steamy smell rising from the charred building. Dick Tozer and the others checked carefully round the offices, making sure all the flames were out. The dog remained with Dick, as if to help him make sure there would be no more fire that night. At last all was safe. The hose-pipes lay coiled like snakes in black puddles of water.

And now, as was his custom, the Prince was handing round cigars to the blackened, weary men. His bearded face looked as black and he appeared as exhausted as the rest, but he was smiling.

Tom Woods had Bob and Betty harnessed again, and *Fire Queen* was on its way back to Chandos Street. Dick Tozer noticed the dog quietly trotting alongside, his head held high. This time there weren't any children or any youths dashing along – they had long ago gone home. In their place was the dog.

Dick Tozer couldn't help a surge of affection for him. Like all at Chandos Street, he was fond of Bob and Betty, Bob in particular, with his tricks and the ways he had of showing off. He liked dogs, too; there were always plenty about, many of them strays. After it had grown out of its puppyhood and was less cuddlesome, some people found a dog a nuisance, and turned it loose on the streets.

This one was different, you could tell that. Perhaps there wasn't anything especially lovable about him; you didn't want to hug him in your arms, he was too big for a start, and, anyway, he looked as if he'd probably give you a nip if you tried. It was his lively personality, his eagerness to be of help, his knowing air of independence which made him so appealing. His alert, shiny, popping eyes searched your face as if he understood every word you said – sometimes he knew what you meant before you'd even said it – and always that puzzled, questioning expression. Sometimes it was sad even, which made you wonder what sort of home he'd once had, where had he come from.

Of course, the dog became the friend of man thousands of years ago – it has existed for at least 10,000 years – of its own choosing, though it may have been influenced in that choice because man provided it with food. Since those first primeval days, no other animal has committed itself to man so much as the dog, offered its affection and undying loyalty. Of all animals the dog is unique. Of all dogs, this one as he trotted along and gave Dick that knowing glance and a short bark as if to say that they were pals who'd work together from now on, was unique. There was something else at the back of Dick's mind, only he couldn't put his finger on it. Something about the dog.

When they got back to Chandos Street, the Prince of Wales himself ordered plenty of beer to be brought in to the fire-station, and saw that the firemen had a good glass each, at his expense. Firemen in those days weren't paid very much, the wage they received was as low as 23s. weekly, so a glass of beer, cheap as it then was, meant a tremendous luxury to them.

The dog looked on as 'Coach' unharnessed Bob and Betty from *Fire Queen*, and led them into the stable at the back of the fire-station, which was number 44 Chandos Street, running into Bedfordbury, part of Covent Garden. The stable backed on to an alley between it and the Coliseum Theatre stage-door. There was plenty of fresh straw, and 'Coach' watered and fed both horses with their favourite food, bran-mash and treacle. Dick Tozer came and saw the dog standing there watching Tom Woods with deep interest, and giving a short little bark every now and again.

'You deserve a juicy bone yourself,' Dick said. And after a few moments he came back with a bone which he had found and gave it to the dog. Soon, he had curled himself up in the straw beside Bob and Betty and fell asleep. He seemed to have taken to them both as if they were life-long friends, just as they had taken to him. Dick Tozer looked in at the stable and saw the dog was asleep. As he gave it a good-night nod, that familiar voice spoke in his ear once again.

'Looks as if he's adopted you,' the Prince of Wales said, and as Dick murmured agreement, went on. 'You should call him Chance, like that dog they had at Watling Street, quite some years ago. He arrived by chance . . .'

It was then that Dick remembered. Now, he knew what it was that had been bothering him. He remembered the story his father had told him about the dog that had found Braidwood in Tooley Street's smoking ruins, to vanish as mysteriously as it had appeared. Some had said it was the ghost of the dog at the old fire-station at Watling Street, that His Royal Highness was referring to. There was an odd, prickling sensation at the back of his neck as Dick recalled how this dog tonight had appeared out of nowhere. How he'd suddenly looked down and he was there. He hadn't been there, and then he was.

'Chance . . .' he said. 'Yes, that's what we'll call him, Your Royal Highness. Chance.'

READY, STEADY, UNDISMAYED

The scene was a station, the time was midnight,
The fatal word 'Fire' on the lamps glittered bright,
The firemen are dozing whilst safely at hand,
The horses are waiting for the word of command.
'Click' goes the message of danger and death,
Down dash the firemen not pausing for breath.
In go the horses – Hi – Hi – clear the way,
While borne on a stretcher a voice seemed to say:

Chorus
Heaven bless the members of the fire brigade,
Heroes true as steel and hearts that are unafraid.
Ready, Steady, Undismayed, are the noble-hearted
Members of the Fire Brigade.

See them arrive at the scene of the fire,
See now the horses they do perspire,
Look at yonder window a woman up there –
Stop – see her falter and then disappear.

Chorus   repeat

This song, *Ready, Steady, Undismayed*, was once a great
favourite at parties, 'socials' and pubs. It was sung by Rose
Paine, born almost next-door to Fire Brigade Headquarters
in Southwark Bridge Road, London S.E.1. She was in her
nineties, when she gave her farewell performance in a song-
competition while on holiday at Margate. As she ended, to
great applause, there came, to her embarrassment, the sound
of fire-engines racing along the front to a devastating fire.

2. Chance's New Friend

30,000 horses are employed in vehicular traffic in London, and 100,000 vehicles pass through the City during twenty-four hours. The numbers are, of course, constantly increasing, as the most superficial observer must have noticed, for the 'press of equine things' in our City thoroughfares is now so great as to form a serious menace to the safety of pedestrianism. One of the biggest – if not the biggest – owners of horses in London is Tilling, of Peckham. They have a stock of about 5,000 animals, they do their own breeding, doctor their own invalids, feed their own family, bring them up in the way they should go, so that when they arrive at a responsible age they shall not depart from it.

The New Penny Magazine, 1885

Telepathy between dog and man has been proved over and over again . . . Never forget that the mentality of one dog is totally different from that of another . . . The dog cannot dissimulate, cannot deceive, cannot lie, because he cannot speak. The dog is a saint.   AXEL MUNTHE

BACK at Tilling's horse-station, that same night, just after ten o'clock the last bus pulled in; the horses were tired and hungry after a long day on London's hard streets, sweat steaming from the pair of them, mingling with the autumn mist which had crept in from Peckham's outlying fields. Both are greys. Years before Thomas Tilling had started his business with one horse, a grey named Kitty, and ever since then the horses he hired out, hundreds of them, to the bus-companies and the fire-brigades, were almost always greys.

The horse-keeper takes charge of the pair of horses, he has a stud of a dozen in his care, and unharnesses them; the driver climbs down from his seat mopping his sweating brow with a large bandana handkerchief; the conductor searches the bus for any dropped coins or lost property.

One of the greys is Bruce. But where is the dog to welcome him? He is disappointed that there is no barked greeting, no welcome for him, as he had become used to during the past weeks. He is led to his stable where he will be watered and given his usual meal, half oats, half maize and hay, but somehow he is less hungry now than he was. The driver, finished for the day, replaces his low-crowned topper and, whip in hand, heads for home, while the conductor puts on his brown bowler and takes his tin cash-box to the office to check the cash against tickets issued.

In his stable Bruce is slow to start tucking into his supper; he feels an odd sensation in his stomach, he is restless. He wishes the dog were there, curled up in the straw at his feet. He misses the dog. There is something in the wind, he knows it, something is going to happen, which has to do with the dog's absence. He doesn't know what it is. But it's something that concerns him.

He hears the contented munching of the other horses on either side of him, and the rustle of straw; the guttering gaslights hiss around the old stable walls, while from the canteen sounds the chatter of the bus-washers as they finish their supper. Quite an army of bus-washers, carpenters and workmen sit over this late-night meal, their job to wash, test and repair each omnibus, making it ready for the road next morning; windows cleaned, wheels tested for loose iron tyres, door-handles and shafts repaired.

On the stable-wall above Bruce's head hung his collar, which was made to measure, no horse's neck being quite the same, and it was as important for a horse-collar to be a good fit as it was for the City man's starched white winged collar. Bruce stood over fifteen hands, he'd been well-fed and cared for, he was strong and hard-working. He possessed the right temperament. When as a five-year-old he first arrived at Peckham over four years ago, Bruce had been put into the hands of Sam Smith, who had harnessed him alongside a horse whose working days were just about done.

Sam Smith had driven them together, carefully, almost tenderly, you might say, through London's streets. For this the driver needed infinite patience and gentlest of hands, and Sam was famous all over London for the way he could train a young horse who, like Bruce, was strong and willing to work, to become accustomed to the bustle of traffic, pedestrians waving umbrellas and all the hazards of London's busy streets.

He had learned not to become scared by the clatter of hansom-cabs, the blare of the German brass bands, the crowded pavements, not to panic at a child's sudden dash across the street under his very hooves. He had learned to keep calm in the noise and clamour all about him, the commotion of a sudden emergency. He had learned to back his load on to a pavement, or turn round in a restricted space.

What he hadn't learned, however, was to foresee the future.

A horse may possess a certain amount of intuition, as much sometimes as that of a human being, or perhaps, even more. But you couldn't expect him to know that this careful training in London's streets, all this teaching and tuition was to fit him not only to become a good bus-horse, but, one day, for something else. A more exciting, more dangerous job.

The job Bruce was to start the very next day.

He couldn't know that this was his last night at Peckham stables, that tomorrow he would be leaving forever. Or did he sense something in the wind? That tingling sensation in his stomach, it may have been due to this intuitive feeling he had. Or might it have been something to do with the dog's absence? He had missed his friendly barks and the way he would settle down in the stall, curling himself up in the straw, with Bruce being careful not to tread on him.

He certainly wasn't able to settle down himself, although it was quiet enough in the stables. The horses on either side of him slept peacefully. Was he restless tonight because his old friend still hadn't shown up? Or was it because of some feeling that something was going to happen?

And then, suddenly, it is five o'clock in the morning, and all is bustle and activity. He had fallen asleep, after all. The chink of harness and he was being groomed, then fed. The veterinary surgeon and his two assistants were busy by half-past five checking the horses' hooves, testing shoes and examining each animal for whip-marks, collar galls, or any other disability which might impair its ability to put in a hard day's work.

That tingling in his stomach. Telling him that

something was going to happen, that it was going to concern him. Then suddenly he wondered – the dog? Where had the dog got to? Why hadn't he turned up?

How was he to know that he and the dog were going to meet again.

Soon.

*

At Chandos Street, later that morning, a thin man in breeches and leggings so shinily polished you could see your face in them, was telling Tom Woods how, the last time he had seen him, old Bob had taken care to prick up his ears, and quite prance about, as if to prove how alert and youthful he was. But Mr Goodwin from Tilling's, for this was who it was, hadn't been deceived for a moment. He had also noticed that Bob's nostrils quivered and his knees trembled slightly, which was a sign that he wasn't feeling as perky as he pretended.

Mr Goodwin, who had a horsy sort of face (perhaps because he had spent such a long time with horses?) and shrewd but kind eyes, was careful to talk quietly. And 'Coach' kept his voice down. They didn't want Bob to overhear their coversation. There wasn't much that went on around the fire-station that he missed; if he realised that there was any thought that he was too old and would have to go, he would feel badly upset.

Mr Goodwin was saying that he had the very horse to take Bob's place, when just at that moment, Chance rushed in, wagging his tail and jumping up at him. 'Why,' he said, 'I've seen that dog before.' He gave Chance a pat. 'Now,' he asked, 'where have we met?'

37

Chance barked again and wagged his tail even more vigorously, Mr Goodwin pushed back his billycock hat and scratched his head and 'Coach' explained to him how the dog had made his appearance at the fire the previous night, and acted with such bravery and sagacity, and how he had been congratulated by the Prince of Wales.

Mr Goodwin stopped scratching his head and straightened his billycock hat. He started to say he wished he could remember where he had seen Chance before, and 'Coach' was about to add that His Royal Highness had thought of his name, when they were interrupted. This time, it was the young girl whom Chance, who turned at once to welcome her, and Dick Tozer had rescued from the office fire. She bent down and put her arms round Chance's neck, exclaiming what a wonderful dog he was. She had brought him a present. 'If it hadn't been for him,' she said to Tom Woods, 'I would have been burned to death.'

'Coach' explained that he had been telling Mr Goodwin all about it. And Mr Goodwin wanted to know what sort of present was it? A nice big bone, no doubt?

'No, it's this,' she said, unwrapping a package she had taken from her coat pocket. It was a dog's collar. But it was no ordinary dog's collar, because, after all, Chance was no ordinary dog. It was a specially big one, with shiny studs and a metal plate for Chance's name to be engraved on it.

'Coach', who got hold of Chance, telling him to be steady, and Mr Goodwin both agreed that it was a fine present, while the girl put the collar round his neck.

Still and steady, Chance stood rather like a soldier about to be decorated with a medal – only being a dog, he had his mouth wide open, tongue hanging out, his bright eyes popping. When the collar was strapped round his neck, he dashed around, barking up at 'Coach' and at Mr Goodwin as if to show them what a wonderful reward he had received, and how much he appreciated it.

Dick Tozer came along to inquire what the noise was all about; he was very pleased to see that the girl had completely recovered from the effects of the fire and also how she had shown her gratitude to Chance. She didn't get much opportunity to say a lot about it because she was interrupted by Chance himself, who, of course, had to jump up at Dick and show off his bright, shining collar as was only to be expected. After all it isn't every day that a dog is given a beautiful collar, even an unusual dog like Chance.

Dick and the girl went off with Chance to show the other firemen the reward he had received, 'Coach' and Mr Goodwin settled what should be done about Bob.

This new horse who would take old Bob's place, a grey, of course, otherwise Mr Goodwin wouldn't have bought him, stood just over fifteen hands, and was a light vanner but with the looks of a Clydesdale, or a Shire about him, though free of hair round the fetlocks. 'Not that looks are all that important,' Mr Goodwin said, and 'Coach' nodded his agreement. This horse had plenty of bone and muscle, which was what was most important, Mr Goodwin pointed out. And short in the leg he was, and very tough.

Tom Woods nodded again. 'Ah – that's important.'

Late that afternoon, Bob's place in the stable, next to Betty, stood empty. He had gone to a new job which had been found for him, with a doctor who lived nearby. A doctor's horse needed to be able to pull up stylishly at patients' houses, accustom itself to waiting outside for long spells – and be pretty impervious to rain. Bob may not have possessed all these qualifications, but the doctor was willing to give him a trial.

Bob would prefer employment on a doctor's round with a smart trap, to retirement at Tilling's old horses' home, Downham Farm at Catford, beyond Peckham, where you could see horses in all stages of sickness or injury being cared for; horses in slings suspended from the ceiling; some wearing a eucalyptus nosebag as an inhalant for bronchial complaints. Or where, when they were old and no longer fit to work, they could end their days peacefully. Bob wasn't the sort who looked forward to spending the rest of his days in peace and tranquillity. He would want to die in harness, as the saying went.

His going had upset the firemen at Chandos Street, who loved him dearly; and Bob himself had played up quite alarmingly. 'Coach' and Dick Tozer and the other firemen had calmed him down, saying that they would come and see him at the doctor's whenever they could. Which seemed to have cheered him up, and off he'd gone.

But what about Chance? How had he acted when Bob had left?

He'd acted quite strangely. Barked and jumped at Bob, bidding him goodbye, and then he had returned to the stable and fussed around Betty, as if trying to comfort her.

But then, his whole attitude had changed. Throughout the afternoon he was restless, getting up from his place in the straw beside Betty, walking round in circles, whining and clicking his teeth. He would trot out into Chandos Street and bark excitedly. He would then dash back into the fire-station, his dark, shiny eyes bulging, which they always did when he was excited. Like at a fire, for instance.

It was as if he was telling everyone that it was something extra special. As one of the firemen said to Dick Tozer: 'It's just as if he knows in advance that something is going to happen.'

Which was rather an extraordinary thing for the fireman to say, as it turned out.

Dick and 'Coach' were awaiting Mr Goodwin when he returned with the new horse. And so was Chance. You should have seen how he behaved the moment he saw the new arrival, he jumped up at him, barking and eyes nearly popping out of his head with excitement. The new horse tossed his head up and down at Chance and pawed the ground with a front hoof.

It was Bruce.

Mr Goodwin could barely make himself heard above Chance's barking. It was then that he said to Dick: 'Why, of course, I knew I'd seen that dog before. It was at the Peckham bus-yard.' He described how, several weeks before, Chance had turned up out of nowhere, and proceeded to make himself at home at the bus-station, straight away becoming Bruce's special friend. Then, yesterday evening, just as suddenly as he had arrived, he had vanished.

Dick Tozer didn't need to hear any more to know who it was had turned up out of the darkness at the fire off Fleet Street last night. 'Why,' he said to 'Coach', 'it's as if he knew beforehand what was going to happen.'

'Ah,' 'Coach' said, 'he'd foreseen how old Bob would go, and how this other horse would take his place, so he'd come on ahead, ready to welcome him.'

'Got second sight, if you ask me,' Dick said.

'Ah,' 'Coach' nodded.

All Mr Goodwin could do was to push back his billycock hat and scratch his head in puzzlement at Chance, who continued to jump up at Bruce, barking his welcome.

Canine intelligence of a high degree is acknowledged the world over, but whether any dog possesses second sight, or any psychic powers for that matter, is something often talked about. As for Chance, the strange way he had attached himself to Chandos Street, and then Bruce following him, was a bit coincidental, not to mention mysterious, and gave Dick Tozer, Tom Woods, and the other firemen quite a lot to talk about. None could know then that Chance was going to puzzle them a good deal more before his story ended.

'Coach' led Bruce quickly into the stable, in Bob's place next to Betty. She gave him her maternal look and nuzzled him affectionately, as if to say she was glad to see him. Characteristically philosophical, she had felt sorry when Bob had left, because they'd been together for quite a number of years. But it was not a ha'porth of use pining for him. Life went on and fires would blaze, and she must work with this new young horse. And that was that.

Mr Goodwin gave Bruce a farewell pat and with a quizzical look at Chance, off he went, still scratching his head and muttering to himself about what strange creatures dogs were, and give him a horse every time.

Bruce settled in right away, and there was no doubt that Chance had made it easy for him to feel at home. He fussed about, dashing to and fro, while Tom Woods saw to it that Bruce was given a meal of bran-mash and treacle as a welcome to Chandos Street Fire Brigade.

The tingling sensation in Bruce's stomach had stopped, his old friend Chance being there to greet him had been a wonderful surprise; quite made him forget to feel homesick for Peckham and the bus-horses.

But his friend had to leave him for a while. Dick Tozer had remembered something he'd heard, probably from his father, about that other dog at the old Watling Street fire-station: how he had worn a collar which had been inscribed with his name on it. He persuaded Chance to let him take his splendid new collar for an hour or so, explaining as best he could that he wanted to have it suitably engraved with his name. Chance grumbled a bit, and growled, and clicked his teeth in that gruesome manner of his, but finally allowed Dick to unstrap his precious collar. Then he insisted on accompanying Dick to the little engraver's shop in New Row, not far distant, up St Martin's Lane.

On the way to New Row Dick walked slowly, trying

to think of something to put on the collar. Chance didn't help very much, he kept on jumping up and dashing ahead, then rushing back, barking at Dick to get a move on – he wanted to return to Chandos Street to see that Bruce was getting along all right.

Just as he turned into New Row, it came to Dick. The man in the engraver's shop listened to him carefully as he explained what he wanted inscribed on the collar.

Chance, who had jumped up on to a rickety chair by the counter, sat motionless and watched with his usual pop-eyed, puzzled expression, as the man bent his spectacles over his engraving-needle and set to work. He was very quick, and when it was done, he refused to let Dick pay for it. Proud to have been of service to a brave fireman, he said. And the fireman's dog. Dick thanked him for his kindness, and Chance added his bark of thanks to the engraver. Dick fastened the collar round his neck, while Chance sat as still and steady as a soldier being decorated for valour.

'There, now everyone will know who you are.' Dick read aloud:

'Stop me not, but onward let me jog,
For I am Chance, the London fireman's dog.'

The engraver's spectacles nodded approvingly, and Chance jumped down from the chair, barking with delight. All the way down St Martin's Lane, he continued to jump up at anyone he met whom he thought ought to know, barking at them as if to say: Look at my wonderful collar with my name on it, and poetry and all to say that I'm no ordinary dog, but Chance, the fireman's dog.

THE FIREMAN

(Sung to the Tune: *God Bless the Prince of Wales*)

The Fireman's life is a dang'rous life!
　Our highest praise he claims:
For he plunges in through the fearful din,
　Where roll the smoke and flames;
He hews down the beam where the fire-sparks gleam,
　He breaks through roof and wall;
Through the blazing door, or the crackling floor,
　He rushes at duty's call.

　　Then give three cheers for the Fire Brigade,
　　　Their noble deeds record;
　　For the dangers that they undergo
　　May Heaven be their reward.

The Fireman's life is a gallant life!
　All dangers will he brave
To rescue mother, father, and child
　From death and a fiery grave.
Oh! never cares he if the perishing be
　Of high or of lowly grade,
Unflinching he goes where the red heat glows;
　Success to each Fire Brigade!

　　Then give three cheers, etc.

The Fireman's life is a noble life!
　And from it we may learn
To do and to dare, be the thing what it may,
　At the call of DUTY stern.
To give up the home for whose quiet ease
We have so stoutly striven,
To part from the friends we have loved for years,
　And leave the result to Heaven.

　　Then give three cheers, etc.

H.W.M.

45

3. Chance Climbs the Social Ladder

The Fire Brigade are happily exhibited with a full dramatic effect, which conveys to the mind of the spectator a vivid impression of reality. The house on fire in the third act, with the burning rafters, the falling shutters, the red glare of the conflagration, the smoke, and cries of the excited mob, and the appearance of the fire-engine in full gear upon the stage, together with the energetic actions of the members of the brigade, bring the excitement up to what Byron would call the grand and sublime climacteric.
Review of 'The Streets of London' by Dion Boucicault at the Adelphi Theatre, London.
The Fireman, 15 August, 1877

There is sorrow enough in the natural way
From men and women to fill our day;
And when we are certain of sorrow in store,
Why do we always arrange for more?
Brothers and Sisters, I bid you beware
Of giving your heart to a dog to tear.
RUDYARD KIPLING

NEXT morning Bruce had settled in, and 'Coach' set about teaching him his fire-drill. At a signal, the alarm went – a mock alarm that a fire had been reported. Bells clanged all over the fire-station. At once Betty shot out to *Fire Queen* and stood waiting to be harnessed up. She knew exactly what to do. It was second nature to her. But Bruce waited in the stable, his eyes rolling, wondering what the noise was all about. Chance barked

47

at his heels, then raced out to where Betty stood, then raced back. Still Bruce didn't seem to understand what was required of him.

'Coach' spoke to him quietly, led him to his place beside Betty and he was harnessed to the fire-engine ready to go. His new harness, different from the one to which as a bus-horse he had been accustomed, allowed him much more freedom; he could lie down when he wished – all that it didn't allow him to do was to face the wrong way round. His collar, instead of the one he'd been used to, was a triced-up spring-clip collar suspended above the fire-engine pole to which, one on either side, he and Betty were harnessed, and it would be lowered into position round his neck and securely locked. If it was left unlocked, a horse could walk right out of his harness. When the fire-alarm rang, or 'the bells went down', as the firemen described it, and the horses went forward, their rugs, secured by toggles, would be left in the air above their places.

After Bruce had gone through the exercise the first time, 'Coach' took him back, together with Betty, to the stable, and the drill was repeated. 'The bells went down' in mock alarm. Chance duly barked as if the fiercest fire ever had been reported; whether he knew it was only practice for Bruce's benefit, you couldn't be sure – though later, in not entirely dissimilar circumstances, it seemed apparent that he did possess foreknowledge of quite startling nature. As before, Betty was in her place and harnessed in a matter of seconds. It didn't take long before, Chance as always barking encouragingly at his heels, Bruce was following

her example. A total of forty seconds it was – no more
– for a turn-out, and he was nicely within the time
allotted.

Then 'Coach' took him, with Betty, out for a
practice run with *Fire Queen*. Bruce knew all about
London crowds and the traffic in the streets, he'd
spent enough years as a bus-horse. Nevertheless, Tom
Woods wanted to know for himself how he behaved
in traffic. He handled the reins gently but firmly, and
he was pleased that Bruce responded as an experienced
horse should.

Bruce, like all horses, was a creature of memory.
That was how he learned. Remembering what he'd
been taught and realising that this was what was
required of him, obeying accordingly. This had been
the way he had been trained ever since he'd been
bought by Mr Goodwin for Thomas Tilling at the
horse-fair on Epsom Downs which takes place every
year during Derby Week, going on until the public
houses closed long after midnight. Everywhere gipsies
and confidential horse-copers, in their smart check
coats and exaggerated breeches; characters with a long
nose, not unlike the horses they were trying to sell,
a permanent wink and about them an odour of stale
spirits.

Tom Woods liked his horses to be a sturdy 15.3
to 16 hands. *Fire Queen* was all of five tons in weight,
and needed pulling, all right; yet a horse hadn't to be
too heavy, for it had to travel like a bat out of hell when
off to a fire. 'Coach' had been compelled to deal with
all manner of horses at Chandos Street; it was part of
the contract with Tilling's that they must be quiet to

drive, good-tempered and without vice. Once there had been a horse named Trix, who when the bells went down would dash forward ready to be harnessed-up, jaws wide open, displaying her teeth, a fearsome sight. She intended no harm to anyone, it was only her eccentric way of displaying her enthusiasm for the job.

'Coach' relied on Mr Goodwin to see that he brought him the right kind of horse – that was what their discussion earlier had been about – and it looked as if Bruce fully answered Mr Goodwin's description. Only one thing he needed now, which was to be re-shod similarly to Betty – very light shoes; a fire-horse was required to run mainly on the natural frog of its hoof, which made them very sure-footed.

From Charing Cross straight down Northumberland Avenue; along Victoria Embankment, *Fire Queen*, with Betty at Bruce's side – and Chance dashing ahead – went at a nice trot. A tug-boat chugging up the Thames to the Pool of London, hooted. The captain of a passing barge waved. Chance barked back; sometimes, eager to encourage Bruce to show Tom Woods how fast he could go, he would run too far ahead. Then he would halt, turn his head with its furrowed questioning brow. 'Come on,' he seemed to be saying, 'Come on, let's see the best you can do.'

'Coach' made no attempt to hurry. Bruce and Betty were keeping a steady pace, she accommodating her stride to his. They reached Westminster Bridge, swung right, then right again into Whitehall, on the way back to Chandos Street. Now Tom Woods shook the reins.

'Giddy-up . . . Giddy-up . . .' Betty responded and

Bruce quickened his pace alongside her. Flying up Whitehall, Betty and Bruce moving as one, their iron shoes struck sparks from the road.

And Chance, caught up in the excitement, barked and raced ahead. By now some small boys were running alongside. Past the grey Home Office building, past Downing Street, where Queen Victoria's Prime Minister, Mr Gladstone, lived. Past the Horse Guards, the guardsmen's plumed helmets and swords glinting, and more and more boys running alongside, shouting encouragement.

London of the eighties was settled, easy-going. Some people might complain of rush and bustle, but for the well-to-do it was all very comfortable. Progress and order moved as Betty and Bruce did, in double harness. Though there was much poverty in the obscure streets off the main thoroughfares, London appeared prosperous. Great hotels off Northumberland Avenue: the Grand, the Metropole, the Victoria; the big shops in Regent Street: Jay's, Peter Robinson's, Dickens & Jones; stores in Tottenham Court Road and Westbourne Grove and Victoria Street, growing ever larger and making it possible to do a day's shopping under one roof.

Now a drizzle of rain started. The traffic was thick, and the wet roads were soon a morass of mud and horse-droppings, which hooves and wheels turned and splashed all over the pavement and shop-windows. Street-orderlies, as they were called, young boys with hand-shovels and brushes, had already appeared, moving among the traffic. Crossing the roads on days like this, except where the crossing-sweeper had made a clean path, made an utter mess of bright boots, and boot-blacks were numerous and did good business.

Bruce's ears at first lay back a trifle self-consciously, then his neck arched, he snorted and his eyes rolled wildly, his heart swelled with a quite natural feeling of superiority as he passed the horse-buses in Whitehall and Trafalgar Square. He knew them in their varied colours: red, blue, yellow, white, green, purple, orange, chocolate – oh, he may not have picked them out by colour, wasn't he colour-blind, after all? – but he knew most horses by sight, those who drew the Favourite, the Atlas, the Royal Blue, the Royal Oak, the Wellington – whose drivers now had an umbrella opened above them, warding off the rain, and advertising some widely used brand of soap or cocoa.

Slowing round the top of Trafalgar Square, *Fire Queen* swung into the Strand. Traffic thickened; ahead lay the famous restaurants, Romano's and Simpson's; theatres and the Tivoli, and beyond Fleet Street – but 'Coach' guided Bruce and Betty left up Adelaide Street into Chandos Street. In a few minutes he was reporting to Dick Tozer and the other fireman that he was well satisfied. Bruce would prove a worthy successor to old Bob.

Increasingly London was becoming more of a fire risk. The popularity of cigarette-smoking resulted in matches and cigarette-ends being thrown aside carelessly, only half put out. In houses packed tightly side by side in over-crowded slums, with hardly room to breathe, an oil-lamp could be knocked over and – whoof! half a street could be a sheet of flame in a matter of minutes.

Early that evening the fire-alarm rang at Chandos Street Station – and no practice turn-out this time – Betty, with Bruce alongside, was quickly in her place and they were rapidly harnessed up. Dick Tozer, 'Coach' and the other firemen were out of the watch-room, buttoning their uniforms, and within a few seconds *Fire Queen* was charging off, the firemen shouting: 'Hi-ya-hi . . .'

But wait a minute. Where was Chance? No encouraging barking at Bruce's heels, no excited jumping up and down and dashing to and fro. The alarm might never have sounded at all, for all the interest he had taken in it. To the amazement of the fireman left on watch, he had remained behind, letting *Fire Queen* depart without so much as a bark, just clicking his teeth in that irritating way he had. Now he crouched by the doors which had been flung wide, head on his paws, with an odd sort of expression which was difficult for any human being to make out. Then suddenly, his ears flicked, his shining eyes popped and he jumped to his feet. As he began barking, *Fire Queen* swept round the corner and with a clash of hooves, Bruce and Betty drew up.

'False alarm,' Dick Tozer shouted. Some irresponsible practical joker had raised the alarm for the fun of it. Disgust and frustration showed on his, 'Coach's' and the rest of the firemen's faces. And then Dick noticed that Chance was wearing what could only be described as a smug expression. Something occurred to him. 'So that's why,' he said slowly, 'you didn't rush off in front.' Mingling wonderment and understanding lit up his face. 'You *knew*.'

Chance jumped up at him, wagging his tail, as if he had followed every word. Dick shouted across to Tom Woods, who was unharnessing Betty and Bruce. 'That's why he didn't come with us – he didn't bother because he *knew* it was a false alarm.'

'Ah . . .' was all 'Coach' could find to say. He stared at Chance and scratched his head in puzzlement, much the same as Mr Goodwin had done.

Less than two hours later, a house in Seven Dials was seen to be on fire. Seven Dials was a slum district in those days, houses and shops packed together at the top of Charing Cross Road. This time when the alarm rang Chance jumped up as if a hat-pin had been stuck into him. He barked and dashed about, and was away like a bullet, as *Fire Queen* raced off. The reflection of the flames in the night sky could be seen from Chandos Street.

'Hi-ya-hi . . .' from Dick Tozer and the firemen, buckling on their belts and axes, and putting on their brass helmets. Bruce's nostrils flared, his hooves pounded the road in unison with Betty's.

It was his first fire.

Chance was almost turning somersaults as he dashed from side to side to keep a clear road; for a moment he would pause, spin on his hind legs under Bruce's head to give him an encouraging bark.

Most dogs, most animals, are terrified of fire. It is a primeval fear.

Why was Chance, on the contrary, fascinated by it? Why should he, like those other strangely individual dogs referred to earlier, feel impelled at the first note of the alarm, to race off to a fire as if his life depended upon it? To train a dog, however intelligent or ready to perform tricks, to face up to a blaze – jump through a hoop of flame, for example – is in most cases when it isn't given up as impossible, acknowledged to be tremendously difficult. Success requires the trainer's endless patience and the dog's utter trust and obedience unto death.

Perhaps it was the noise, the pandemonium, that sent Chance tearing off? The clamour of the fire-alarm, the shouts, the rushing, yelling crowd, the sound of horse's hooves that charged his blood with excitement, set his nerves ajangle?

Or was it more to do with the fact that he was with Bruce and Betty? Dogs are known to form special attachments for horses. At a racing-stable, for instance, a particular dog will choose a particular horse for a friend, and remain faithful to it in quite a remarkable way. This may have been the case with Chance and helps to explain perhaps his strange behaviour over Bruce, his uncanny foreknowledge that he, of all the bus-horses at Tilling's, would be taking old Bob's place.

Now, from Seven Dials, Chance could scent the acrid smell of burning; about him rose the roar of the crowd rushing towards the sinister glow above the rooftops, the yells of ragged bare-footed children who swarmed London's streets.

Horse-buses, hansom-cabs and private carriages made way for *Fire Queen*, bicycles took care to keep out of the way – even that most reckless, the evening paper cyclist, who delivered the various editions from Fleet Street to the street news-stands. When the racing results were through, his career through the streets was a phenomenon; with half-a-hundredweight of papers on his back, he would scorch under the horses' heads, and dodging through an eighteen-inch space between buses, he was as much a trick-cyclist as any music-hall performer.

Fire Queen had reached the top of Charing Cross Road. Glittering harness and gleaming brass helmets. Bruce and Betty going all out. Chance zigzagging and barking all the time. The firemen's crescendo yells. 'Hi-ya-hi . . .'

Now they were in an area thronged with criminals, house-breakers, cracksmen, footpads, street thugs and 'bug-hunters', as they were called, who used to hang around public houses, cleaning out drunks' pockets; pick-pockets, thieves known as 'snoozers' who robbed hotel-guests, women who enticed children into their houses and stripped them of their clothes, who were called 'skinners'; and gamblers with cogged dice, and a whole variety of villains.

A cloud of black smoke was pouring out of a street as Tom Woods urged Bruce and Betty on. But Bruce began to slow when he smelt the smoke. It frightened him – he'd never met fire and smoke before. 'Coach' had to start cracking the whip above his head, making sure though that it never actually touched the horse. Bruce kept going, but only because Betty was pulling so hard alongside him.

They turned a corner. The house that had caught alight was narrow, every room crowded with a family, and it would quickly set other houses around it ablaze. 'Coach' saw that Bruce was frightened, and he

shouted: 'We'll push it the rest of the way.' Jumping down he quickly unharnessed the horses, Bruce first. He always did this at a fire so that he could lead them to safety. But he didn't fully realise how frightened Bruce was by the smoke and the flames leaping up the walls of the house.

He turned to Betty. The moment Bruce felt free, he bolted. Back down the street away from the fire he galloped, ears pricked back and the whites of his rolling eyes showing.

Tom Woods could only gape; but Chance shot after Bruce, barking for all he was worth. When he heard Chance behind him, Bruce slowed down. Chance caught up with him and tore round in front, bringing him to a standstill, grabbing the end of a trailing rein in his mouth. He pulled Bruce's head round. Then, giving an occasional growl of encouragement, led him back towards the fire.

Tom Woods took the rein. This time Bruce followed him obediently, shaking his head and sneezing from the effects of the smoke; but he showed no signs of wanting to run away again. 'Coach' led him away to join Betty further down the street. Tom Woods had found it difficult to believe what he'd seen, and Dick Tozer, other firemen, and onlookers had stood open-mouthed as they watched Chance rush after Bruce and coolly bring him back.

The fire was dealt with speedily and efficiently – other fire-engines were on the scene quickly after *Fire Queen* – the threatened holocaust averted. Jack While, plus note-book and pencil-stub, obtained his 'fire-copy' as usual and rushed it off to Fleet Street. Captain Shaw expressed himself well pleased with his men, and after hearing of Chance's resourcefulness in saving Bruce from blotting his copy-book at his first fire, gave him a congratulatory pat, receiving a bark in return.

*

A fireman's life was not all fighting fires, drama and danger, excitement and tragedy. There were the routine tasks day in, day out, to be taken care of. *Fire Queen* washed down first thing every morning, and not an inch of brasswork that wasn't made to shine; 'Coach' saw to it, too, that as well as Bruce and Betty being groomed each day, their harness was brightly polished.

Firemen were used to keeping everything ship-shape, so to say, for Captain Shaw insisted that every man jack of them should have served as sailors in the Royal Navy or as merchant-seamen. 'A sailor is used to being called upon at all times, night or day, climbing, running up and down ladders, and a few years at sea makes him quick, alert and ready for any emergency. And,' he would add, 'they don't take harm after a good wetting, either.'

Dick Tozer, for instance, had like his father before him, gone to sea aged ten. Been all round the world more than once. Served on a whaler, he had, in the South Antarctic; and life came no tougher than in a whaling-vessel. Like his fellow firemen, beginning training, he'd been attached to drill and instruction classes at Southwark headquarters for three months, during which time he hadn't been allowed to take part in an actual turn-out, but went along to any serious fire in charge of an instructor, to help all he could and gain first-hand experience.

Passing through the drill class, he had remained attached to headquarters only temporarily, before he was drafted to Chandos Street, where strict routine became almost all of his life.

6.45 a.m.	Call hands.
7.00 a.m.	Relieve station duty and commence general work.
8.00 a.m.	Breakfast.
8.45 a.m.	Make beds.
9.00 a.m.	Muster.
9.00–9.15 a.m.	Clean uniform.
9.15 a.m.	Tell off as requisite.
11.00 a.m.	Stand easy 15 minutes.
1.00 p.m.	Dinner, when work should be finished.
7.00 p.m.	Relieve station duty.
9.00 p.m.	Muster and escape duty commences.
10.00 p.m.	All lights turned down and station doors closed.

All hands to be properly cleaned within one hour of work being finished.

This routine was subject to alterations under special circumstances, but as a general rule had to be complied with.

Relief from duty did not mean that Dick's time was then his own; he was on duty throughout the twenty-four hours of the day, and was taken off one job and put on another. Leave of an hour or two could be granted only in special circumstances; one week's holiday, plus a total of no more than twenty-six full days off, was all that was allowed during the year.

Dick was unmarried and lived at the fire-station,

paying one shilling weekly rental, married firemen were allocated quarters at a nominal rental. Single men were detailed off weekly as cook and caterer, and excused from attending fires by day.

As well as fire-stations there were street escape-stations, or watch-boxes, sited in various parts of London which were provided with gas, water and drainage, and equipped with fire-fighting appliances and a hand-worked escape-ladder. Upon receiving report of a fire the fireman on duty pulled the street-alarm nearby and turned out with the escape, obtaining the assistance of any passers-by he could, for which he was allowed to pay one shilling per person for their services. While on duty a fireman was allowed to lie down and sleep in his watch-box, but must be in full uniform with the exception of his helmet, and, as at the fire-station itself, must be inside and the door shut at 10.00 p.m.

In addition to his fireman duties Dick Tozer now had to keep Chance looking spruce. He would get a bucket of warm water, a slab of strong soap, and give Chance a bath, always very careful not to get the soap in his eyes. Chance would click his teeth and growl and grumble as if he hated his bath-night. After being thoroughly dried with a rough towel, he would rush round, jumping up and shaking himself, barking and making a terrible fuss, as if to say: Never again, that was the last time Dick would ever get him to take a bath. But he did put up with it every week, and though he would growl and grumble going through the same performance each time, Dick began to suspect that really he quite enjoyed bath-times.

Chance felt great affection for Dick, no doubt, even if he couldn't be said to go out of his way to show it. That is to say he didn't play games, didn't express any signs of love which many dogs express to their owners. Perhaps it was because Dick hadn't owned him from a puppy; a fact which aroused considerable speculation concerning his antecedents, many wondered if he ever had been a puppy at all. His personality was so mature, his expression worried and wise, added to his uncanny knack of being able to see into the future, made it difficult, even Dick admitted it, to believe that he had ever possessed the characteristics of a cuddlesome, playful, innocent-eyed pup.

Not only did he unerringly know when an alarm-call was false or not – though the firemen couldn't take advantage of his foreknowledge thus saving themselves the trouble of rushing off for nothing, just in case this time it was the real thing – but he knew, hours before-hand, when he was due to be given his bath, for example. By the time hot water, bath and soap were ready he would have contrived to make himself scarce. Dick would take several minutes calling for him without any reply, which for Chance was most unusual, ordinarily he was not exactly backward in reminding everyone of his presence. Then, suddenly, he would be there, Dick would find himself staring down at that worried expression, and after some self-conscious behind-wriggling and tail-wagging, the business of bathing him would get under way.

When it was a genuine turn-out he would, without fail, dash out, and unhesitatingly turn right or left along the correct street that *Fire Queen* must take to reach the fire. He knew where it was. Invariably, too, he knew an hour beforehand when the Skipper was going to show up on his round of inspection. His manner would become somewhat subdued, almost decorous, he would dart in and out of the fire-station, staring hard in the direction whence Captain Shaw would appear, and several minutes before the carriage drew up he would bark and jump about, click his teeth and generally convey the news of the fire-chief's imminent arrival.

Cleaning and polishing *Fire Queen*, the fire-station itself kept neat and tidy as a new pin, and every man on his toes, prepared for any emergency, serving long hours of duty, sleeping in their uniforms, ready to answer any alarm-call promptly, whatever the hour, all this was daily routine. In addition – regular fire-drill, which was when Captain Shaw put into practice his belief in the importance of promoting the achievements of London's fire-service in the eyes of the public.

Perhaps he was a bit of a social climber, but he used his upper-crust connections to secure the interest of the Prince of Wales and his set, in the work of the fire-brigade. Where they led the general public would follow. To this end, the Prince and other notables had a long-standing invitation to Wednesday fire-drill.

The future Edward VII had been a fire-fighting enthusiast ever since he had witnessed his first fire, aged eleven, when the Prince of Wales Tower blaze at Windsor Castle had been dealt with so smartly by Braidwood: twelve years later Marlborough House caught fire, this was extinguished, according to Jack While's father, mainly by the Prince's exertions (though, trusting to lath and plaster, he fell partly through the ceiling).

What attracted the Prince to fire-fighting was his predilection for colourful uniforms – he was highly clothes-conscious, changing his attire several times a day, owning a wardrobe of suits and coats; an honorary admiral or general of most of Europe's fleets or armies, he was the proud possessor of innumerable uniforms and sashes, epaulettes and belts, buckles, swords, feathers and other regalia. None was more precious than the uniform, pressed and cleaned after every fire, in which he would emerge from Chandos Street Fire Station, complete with axe, belt and silver helmet, off to some promising conflagration. Short and plump, with bulging eyes and rather weak chin hidden by a beard, he nevertheless cut a dashing figure as Fireman No. 116.

The Prince, as well as several friends, including the Duke of Sutherland, Lord Arthur Somerset and the Duke of Marlborough, themselves keen amateur fire-fighters, took great delight in encouraging the professionals by their august presence. The man-in-the-street was there, too, lending popular support to the occasion. Jack While reported how the regular Wednesday afternoon displays, which the Prince and his friends attended whenever they could, became so famous that carriages and crowds often jammed Southwark Bridge Road. Tickets had to be obtained far in advance if you wanted to get in to see the entertainment.

Southwark headquarters-drill-yard was overlooked on one side by Winchester House, Captain Shaw's home and offices, on the other side by a converted warehouse, accommodating the firemen and their families. Moving there from Watling Street, E.C.4, when he took command in 1878, the Skipper and his family occupied the twenty-room house, once St Saviour's Workhouse, but entirely re-built.

Described by the ubiquitous Jack While as 'the largest and handsomest fire-station yet erected and of the style that is now becoming familiar for that purpose – namely florid Gothic in red brick and stone facings – but set in the midst of a somewhat low class neighbourhood', the drawing-room boasted a coloured print, *The Rescue* (a copy of it adorned most fire-stations at the time) depicting a fireman rescuing two children from a burning building. On the dining-room wall, Millais's more famous picture, featuring a real-life fireman, named Hodges, also engaged in a dramatic rescue, and also entitled *The Rescue*.

Outside a wooden balcony and stairway led to the drill-yard. From this vantage-point the Prince of Wales and a party of friends, together with Captain Shaw, his wife and two children, watched the training display attended that Wednesday afternoon by Chandos Street Fire Brigade, *Fire Queen*, Bruce and Betty and all. And, of course, Chance; as it transpired it was to prove to be quite an occasion for him.

He'd been given his bath the previous night especially for this afternoon, and here he was jumping around as usual, making himself conspicuous, you might say, determined that the Prince would remember him from that night when he had attached himself so dramatically to Dick Tozer and the Chandos Street Fire Brigade.

'Coach' had led out Bruce and Betty with *Fire Queen*, their well-groomed glossy grey coats much admired, and the Prince, who had learned that old Bob was now drawing a doctor's trap and his place taken by a new horse, spoke to Bruce, and one of the elegantly dressed ladies at his side gave him a lump of sugar.

Chance was putting up such a performance that the Prince couldn't help noticing him. Part of his job as future King was never to forget a face, and although you may say it was only a dog's face, Chance was no ordinary dog and the Prince, who loved dogs – one of his own, Caesar, was to become world-famous when, years later, he walked alone at his beloved owner's funeral – deliberately teased Chance by affecting to ignore him.

Chance almost jumped out of his skin in ever more frantic attempts to attract His Royal Highness's notice. Finally, the Prince gave him a good pat and admired the collar round his neck inscribed with the name he had himself suggested. Chance relaxed somewhat, though he strutted around proudly and clicked his teeth – until the incident occurred which was to deflate him, temporarily at any rate.

The display began with Captain Shaw explaining, not to the Prince who knew all about it, but to the rest, how *Fire Queen* operated. The fire-box fixed beneath the vehicle was stoked up to heat the water-tank, this produced the steam to drive the pumps which forced the water through the hose-pipe directed at the flames.

The Chandos Street firemen sent a great jet of water high into the air, the ladies gave little screams of excitement, and one of the gentlemen's top hats became caught in a gust of wind, and fell. Chance retrieved it before it bowled into a puddle of water. The gentleman was delighted and amazed that Chance's teeth, which looked sharp enough when he barked, hadn't marked the hat in the slightest.

Next, the escape-ladder was wheeled out to demonstrate how a fireman could climb up and rescue a victim caught high up in a burning building. A young recruit stepped forward, name of Jimmy Draper, who had spent all his life at sea. While in Sydney his ship, the *Orient*, lay close to *H.M.S. Bacchante*: on board were the Prince of Wales' sons, the Duke of Clarence and the Duke of York. They had made an inspection of the *Orient* during their fire-fighting display. The Duke of York had gone out of his way to congratulate young Draper: 'I would strongly advise you if you are seeking a future career, to join the London Fire Brigade, because my father happens to know the Chief Officer, Captain Shaw, who is taking on only sailors as firemen.'

Some time later, in 1880, Draper home from the sea, stayed in a house in Poplar which caught fire, and the fire-brigade's handling of the blaze so impressed him that with the Duke of York's advice in mind he had sought out Captain Shaw. He was forthwith put through a series of tests, the first, called 'The Fatal Leap', entailed jumping out of a window thirty feet into a jumping-sheet; he passed this and the rest successfully and was duly posted to Chandos Street.

Now the moment arrives for him to ascend the fire-escape. He starts up. Somehow, it rises much higher than it had ever done before. He gives a gulp as he watches – up and up shoots the fire-escape to disappear like a church-steeple, almost, it seems to him in his sudden nervousness, vanishing into a cloud. He feels the perspiration form on his brow, start to trickle down the side of his face. Ordinarily he had no fear of heights, hadn't he spent years climbing ship's rigging under most dangerous circumstances? And he had passed climbing the escape-ladder test easily. It is simply the sudden realisation that this isn't any ordinary occasion – this time the eyes of the Prince of Wales and all these fine Society people are on him.

He hears the command to ascend as if it comes from far away. He tries to pull himself together; he grits his teeth. Then, a sharp bark behind him and a roar of laughter, as Chance rushes past and up the escape-ladder, climbing with the assurance of an experienced fireman. Yet, no-one had ever seen him perform the feat before. Draper watches, struck with amazement, as Chance, tail wagging – whether to help him keep his balance or to show everyone how pleased he is with himself, you couldn't tell – reaches the top.

A burst of applause from all below. It breaks off suddenly. Everyone freezes. Something is the matter with Chance. A gasp of dismay from everyone. He can't get down. He had climbed up to the top all right, but he can't descend backwards, nor can he turn round and descend head first. He is stuck where he is.

What must have been poor Chance's thoughts? There is little doubt that, eager as he always was to help anyone, he had climbed the ladder to encourage the recruit, to show him there was nothing to it. As a result he had got himself into this predicament. His teeth were clicking like anything. Not because he was frightened of falling and being killed, he didn't know anything about death so he couldn't fear it, he didn't fear anything, but he must have felt furious at having made such a fool of himself. Dogs hate being made to look fools, even the most ordinary dog which Chance was far from being, and it was worse for him. He gave a bark which turned into a pathetic yelp. At the same time a roar of applause again, and he gave a quick, nervous look below.

The moment young Draper realised that Chance was in difficulty, he forgot his own momentary fright, and now he was climbing the ladder – up, up, he went, without a thought for his previous fear. He heard the applause but didn't glance down, He threw a look up at Chance.

'All right. Stay where you are.'

Chance's half bark and half whimper indicated that he had no intention of doing anything else but follow this advice. Draper balanced himself – he didn't even think about how high he was – reached up and grabbed Chance with one hand. Coolly and calmly, just as any experienced fireman would.

Chance's eyes popped, he wagged his tail energetically as the recruit tucked him under his arm. Down they went, to be greeted with cheers and congratulations from the Prince of Wales, Captain Shaw and Dick Tozer and all. Chance was petted and made a great fuss of by the Society ladies, which he much enjoyed; nearly turning somersaults he jumped up at his rescuer and licked his face with a very slobbery tongue, to show his gratitude. But Draper knew it was the other way round. It was he who felt grateful to Chance.

For that one paralysing moment of indecision his self-confidence had faltered. Without any thought for himself or anyone else – he hadn't cared about the Prince and the swells looking on, not he – Chance had set a blood-tingling example, which Draper had felt impelled to follow.

Now came the climax of the afternoon. A real fire. This was started in the yard in a section of a house specially provided for drill purposes. Another recruit was detailed to demonstrate his resourcefulness, a heavily-moustached chap, of weather-beaten countenance and jaunty personality, named Perceval. He had proved a bit of a surprise-packet from the start when, dressed in a closely buttoned frock coat, and top hat, he had applied to join the fire-brigade. Trained as a naval cadet in the *Worcester* at Greenhithe, he claimed, producing his papers; sailed on ships bound for India and the Far East, and obtained his second mate's ticket; but tiring of the sea, he had determined to become a fireman. In the drill-yard he was required single-handed to elevate the escape-ladder from horizontal to vertical position. Unconcernedly, with effortless ease he had proceeded to raise the escape, and turning to Captain Shaw, who was looking on, he said: 'I could have done it on my blinking head.' He was recruited on the spot.

The flames in the realistic simulation of a house afire were now burning fiercely, and Perceval was instructed to dash in, as if effecting a rescue. With confident enthusiasm he set about smashing in the door with his axe. Smash, hack . . . Smash, hack . . . Dick Tozer stepped forward, stopped him, and calmly turning the door-handle, opened the door to a roar of good-natured laughter from all sides. After a moment's surprise and chagrin, Perceval joined in the laughter himself. It was an old trick which was played on every recruit, to teach him to make sure that a door was unlocked and would open without any need to smash it in with his axe.

The display ended with *Fire Queen* heading back to Chandos Street, while Captain Shaw showed the Prince of Wales and his party into the drawing-room for tea.

THE FIRE BRIGADE

Our soldiers and sailors are gallant and brave,
And they well serve their Queen on the land and the wave,
With nerves that are strong, and with hearts that are true,
And we gladly give honour where honour is due.

But, to-night, I would ask you to think upon those
Who go forth to fight the most deadly of foes,
Who boldly risk danger and death undismayed,
Then let's have a toast for the Fire Brigade!

When the terrible flames are extending around,
And no other succour or help can be found,
Our wives and our children are saved by their aid,
And our blessings are breathed for the Fire Brigade!

With their lives in their hands, they advance to the spot,
Though the rafters are creaking, and walls are red-hot,
And the march of the cruel destoyer is stayed
By the daring and skill of the Fire Brigade!

Their hardships are many, but firm are their ranks,
And well by their conduct they merit our thanks;
Their deeds are heroic, and never shall fade;
Three cheers and one more for the Fire Brigade!

WILLIAM GURNER, 15th August 1877

4. Chance and the Dancing Bear

A horse is a noble animal, but he does not always do so.
Schoolboy's essay

Horrible, hairy, human, with paws like hands in prayer,
Making his supplication rose Adam-zad the Bear!
I looked at the swaying shoulders, at the paunch's
    swag and swing,
And my heart was touched with pity for the monstrous,
    pleading thing.
                                        RUDYARD KIPLING

There is no faith which has never yet been broken,
except that of a truly faithful dog.
                                        KONRAD LORENZ

JACK WHILE, as usual at the display, scented a story
in Perceval, and remaining behind at Southwark headquarters found him in the billiards-room near the
watch-room, where the firemen could spend the time
while waiting for the alarm. Over a game of billiards
While learned that the new recruit's full name was
Arthur Augustus Perceval, but he preferred to be
called 'Gussie'. He had married a barmaid at the
Criterion, named Kate – who was in fact an American
girl from South Carolina. 'There's nothing I like better
than a pint of old and mild, which is how I met her,
got the best beer in London at the Cri.'
His story was interrupted by the entrance of the

73

Prince of Wales, who hadn't returned with his friends to Marlborough House, but wanted a game – he often looked in for a game of billiards with anyone who was free to play. It was due to his interest in the firemen's welfare that the Queen had recently sent complete sets of Dickens, Walter Scott, Shakespeare and Thackeray, for the fire-station library, together with autographed copies of her own books, *Leaves from the Journal of Our Life in the Highlands* and *More Leaves from the Journal of Our Life in the Highlands.*

The Prince took on Gussie, and Jack While realised that the new fireman was the nephew of the Earl of Egmont, and moreover he would himself one day inherit the title. An heir to an earldom becomes a fireman – here was a story and no mistake. Gussie was to prove himself as brave as any of his comrades and did, in fact, inherit the title in 1897.

Meanwhile, back at Chandos Street Dick Tozer, 'Coach', Jimmy Draper and the rest relaxed in the watch-room, discussing the afternoon's events, especially Chance's performance up the escape-ladder. Chance was spread out at Dick's feet, contributing every now and then with a bark to the conversation. The firemen were spinning yarns of the hazards of their life; how at a fire off Aldgate High Street, several years before, the heat had been so intense it had shrivelled up the leather helmets they then used. Captain Shaw had recently returned from Paris, where he had noted the brass helmets, with feathery decorations, worn by the *Sapeurs-Pompiers*, the fire-brigade, which was part of the French Army. Forthwith, dispensing with the feathers, the Skipper provided his men with

74

brass helmets, for their better protection.

Then the alarm rang. All leapt up, Chance barking away, and reached for jackets, helmets, belts and axes. Betty and Bruce were already in their places harnessed to *Fire Queen*. 'Coach', as he climbed quickly into his seat, thought he noticed something slightly amiss with Betty, but in the rush and clamour of the moment, it had gone. It was to be brought back to his mind later.

Fire Queen's great iron-shod wheels rattled out of the fire-station. 'Hi-ya-hi . . .' from Dick Tozer and the rest of the firemen, the horses' hooves pounding through the traffic, they sped up towards Holborn. A sinister reddish glow could be seen above the dark roof tops, Chance was out front, his warning barks helping to clear the way. By now, a score of boys and youths were racing alongside, adding their excited shouts to the commotion, some bare-footed, their feet splashing through puddles, while others, out for a good time in London by night, wore their best suits; a fire was a bonus excitement not to be missed.

Bruce had quickly settled down to his new job, and was pulling strongly. Whatever might have been wrong with Betty just before she set out was no longer apparent to 'Coach'. The half-query which had flashed across his mind was forgotten.

'Giddy-up . . . Giddy-up . . .'

He let Betty and Bruce have their heads, they needed no urging as, nostrils flaring and eyes rolling with excitement, they careered through a huddle of streets at the back of Drury Lane, which looked more like a fair-ground or market. Hundreds of stalls, each with its own illumination, naphtha-lamps, or the red smoky flame of old-fashioned grease lamps. One fishmonger had stuck candles in bundles of wood shining over yellow haddocks; candles flamed in huge turnips, tallow guttering over the sides, where a boy was shouting: 'Eight a penny, pears.'

Night-workers grouped round a coffee-stall joined the cheers as *Fire Queen* raced past, with clattering wheels and yelling youngsters; and faces appeared at upstairs windows, one old man leaning out so excitedly that his nightcap fell off and floated down like a small balloon.

At a corner, a horse and a trap stood outside a house. The policeman on his beat noted that the same horse and trap had stood there the previous evening; they belonged to a doctor on his nightly visit to a patient.

As the policeman stopped to give the horse a friendly tug at his grey mane, he saw the tell-tale glow in the sky above the house opposite. A fire several streets away, he decided. The horse gave a jerk of his head and whinnied.

'Hello? What's up, then?'

The horse began to tremble, replied with another whinny and pawed the ground. At that moment, *Fire Queen* came rushing up the street, the shouting mob alongside it and the horse reared up, whinnying more loudly. The door of the house opened, the doctor stood outlined in the light from the hall, clutching his black bag and stethoscope. He hurried down the steps, his mouth open to ask what was the matter.

'Hi-ya-hi . . . Hi-ya-hi . . .'

Then it happened. His whinny rising into a high-pitched scream, the doctor's horse swung round, taking the trap with him, and chased after the fire-engine.

'Come back . . .' shouted the doctor. 'Come back . . .'

But you've already guessed – yes, it was old Bob. Hearing *Fire Queen* again like that had proved too much for him. His thoughts flew back to when he and Betty were together, chasing off to a fire. Round the corner he charged, whinnying at the top of his voice, as if to say: 'Wait for me – wait for me . . .' The trap swung dangerously from side to side. It seemed it must turn over. But on he went – nothing could stop him – on, on.

'Hi-ya-hi . . . Hi-ya-hi . . .'

The crowd shouting and the familiar smell of fire, and Bob's nostrils flared, eyes rolled, the doctor's trap swayed wildly behind him.

The blazing house came into sight, flames licking the roof, smoke filling the night sky. *Fire Queen* went into action, the hose-pipe snaking out, the powerful jet of water spraying the flames. Now the crowd made way for Bob. What was this old horse doing here, with an empty trap?

'Coach' had taken Betty and Bruce down the street out of danger, and he turned, astonished, as Bob rushed up. Quickly he went and grabbed his bridle. 'Steady, Bob, steady.' Bob whinnied. 'All right, old chap.'

Bob's eyes stopped rolling. He was in a lather of sweat and trembling all over. 'Coach' calmed him, patting his neck affectionately. He'd heard tales of fire-horses who'd been retired to a milk-round or a butcher's cart, even drawn the mayor's carriage, and had joined in when a fire-engine had rushed past, but it had never happened to one of his horses. He led Bob away from the fire. He would unharness him until after the fire before returning him to the doctor.

But as he reached for the reins entangled with the shafts, he felt Bob give a dreadful shiver. Something was wrong, and instinctively he moved to the old horse's head. He was too late. Bob began sinking to his knees, and then toppled over.

He was dead.

Tom Woods stared down at him, tears brimming his eyes. He knelt and lifted the grey, noble head. 'You died in harness,' he muttered, a choking sensation in his throat. 'Even,' he went on, 'if it was in a doctor's trap.' He felt a cold nose beside him and there was Chance, his head low, his tail dropping. 'Coach' gave him a pat. 'It was the way he would have wished to go. To die in harness at a fire . . .'

The fire came under control and *Fire Queen* returned to Chandos Street. 'Coach' fed and watered Bruce and Betty; he, Dick Tozer and the other firemen felt upset over old Bob, so that he hardly noticed that Betty didn't eat up with her usual appetite. In the commotion of rushing to the fire, he'd forgotten the fleeting impression he had received earlier, that she wasn't in her usual bright spirits. Now, had he thought there was something wrong, he would have put it down to Betty feeling upset about Bob.

What, he asked Dick Tozer and the others, would happen to Bob? Off to the knacker's yard, that was his fate, like most horses' when they died, seventy per cent of them, thoroughbreds or cart-horses; a horse's working-life in London was not long, averaging out at five years. Bus-horses fared better, they were well looked after, and could do their four to five years and then be strong enough to go to the fire-brigades. Even so, a larger percentage of bus-horses were sold to slaughter at £5 a piece, two or three thousand a year.

London's best-known horse-slaughterer then was Jack Atchelor in Wandsworth, who turned the carcases over to a firm named Harrison, Barber & Company at Garrett Lane, Wandsworth. This huge factory disposed of some 25,000 worn-out horses every year, this was in the days when London teemed with horses, some 50,000 of them. Bones sold for buttons or artificial fertiliser; hooves converted into glue; shoes resold to blacksmiths; and tails and manes used in upholstery or for fishing-lines. The hides were the most valuable part of the carcase, and had many uses. Notably as weatherproof covering for the very carriages a horse might until recently have been pulling about the streets. Then the sale of horse-meat. A horse in good condition would yield two and a half hundredweight, a great market for which was in the East End, where butchers made up a pound of meat in six ha'porths.

Tom Woods, Dick Tozer, young Draper and the rest of the firemen shook their heads sadly at the thought that this was the end that poor old Bob would come to. Bob deserved a decent burial, they thought. It was decided to get the money with which to provide him with one, and Captain Shaw, who called to inquire about what had transpired, agreed. There and then, he made the first contribution. The others, ill-paid though they were, and some had wives and children to keep, added what they could. But how were they going to find the rest of the money needed?

Dick had an idea. Why not send out Chance with a collecting-box? That ought to raise a bit of money. In those days it was not an uncommon sight to see a dog at Charing Cross Railway Station, for example, collecting money for charity. Chance, who had been enjoying a snooze during the discussion, woke up the moment he heard his name mentioned. He gave Dick Tozer a bark as if to ask what it was all about.

'You're going to collect some money so that old Bob can rest in a peaceful grave.'

Next day, a collecting-box was strapped on to Chance's back. Dick Tozer wrote out on a piece of cardboard what money was needed to give old Bob, the fire-horse, a decent burial. 'Give generously,' he wrote in large letters, and the card was tied round Chance's neck, who barked excitedly, his shiny eyes popping, and dashed out of the fire-station, looking up and down Chandos Street. He stared back at Dick and the others watching him. His brow wore its usual worried furrows. He was obviously deep in thought.

'Off with you,' Dick said, 'and get some money for poor old Bob.'

Chance regarded him with an injured air as if to say: 'Oh, I know exactly what you want me to do . . . Just give me a moment to make up my mind where I start.' Then he turned, paused to glance back – he wanted to make sure that all eyes were on him as he made his exit – and trotted into the street.

As he went off, Dick said to 'Coach': 'You'd think that going out and collecting money was a daily occupation with him.'

The firemen often took Chance to their homes, to show him off to their wives and children and the neighbours. As a result he had become well-known all round the Charing Cross area. Hansom-cab drivers, lamplighters and messenger-boys, postmen and the newspaper-sellers, bootblacks and shopkeepers, all knew him and he knew them.

Off now he went to make the rounds of his friends; he stopped people he knew in the street, the hawker of cat's meat, the cane-chair mender on the kerb; the hawker with pot-flowers ('all a-blowing and a-growing') the man with the gravel cart: ('Gravel your garden path') and the journeyman glazier looking about for broken window-panes.

Chance stopped every mother's son, even if he didn't know them very well, he stood in their path until he heard the chink of a coin in the collecting-box. Or he would click his teeth in that awful way he had, putting anyone else's teeth on edge until they dropped a coin into the box. When it began to fill, he'd stop anyone who was a bit slow and shake himself so that the coins rattled invitingly. Whoever it was, always took the hint.

He was careful not to jump up as he did ordinarily, for fear that the collection-box might slip off and he would lose it. Here was a one-man-band, a familiar figure in the side-streets, who carried musical pipes fixed under his mouth, a drum on his back which he beat with a stick tied to his elbow, cymbals on the top

of the drum which he clashed by a string attached to
to his heel, and a triangle in his hand. Even he was
forced to stop and find a coin.

It was as he made his way along the Strand, dodging
up side-streets whenever he saw anyone whom he
thought would be useful to give him a coin, that he
saw the dancing bear.

It seemed huge to him. It stood, in fact, higher than
its owner who was a dark-eyed, sallow individual with
a large waxed moustache. It was the first dancing bear,
or bear of any kind for that matter, that Chance had
ever come across, though there were quite a number of
them in London, brought over from the Continent.
Held by a strong chain attached to a heavy steel collar
round its neck, the bear was tightly muzzled. It was
supposed to be unpredictable, likely as not to bite
anyone at any time – although bears were popular
street-attractions, always drawing a crowd when they
performed a sort of dance to their owner's violin or
tune played on a bugle, they weren't regarded as tame.

Chance paused as he stood in front of the bear.
Suddenly his eager, questioning expression softened,
those popping, shiny eyes seemed sad; his mouth
opened as he turned his head slightly on one side.
Something about this large, clumsy-looking creature,
fur shaggy and unkempt, touched some chord within
Chance. Its owner started to lead it away, and Chance
barked at him. His whole attitude changed; he was
no longer concerned with collecting money, but darting
round bear and man, it seemed as if he was trying to
head them off. He didn't want the bear to proceed in
the direction the man was going. But the collection-box

on his back was proving too heavy and impeded him. With one loud bark at the man he trotted off, his expression that of one who had done his best, but if his help wasn't wanted, well, there was nothing more he could do about it.

He was destined to meet the dancing bear once again.

He returned to the job of raising money for Bob. He decided to cross the Strand to Charing Cross Railway Station. The heavy traffic made it dangerous, but he knew the policeman who was on duty – he knew all the policemen in that particular area – and barked loudly to attract his attention. The bobby saw him waiting on the kerb, and with a grin, held up his hand. Obediently, horse-buses and hansoms, carriages and vans, came to a sudden halt. Just as if frozen for the moment into a great marvellous photograph.

Only Chance moved as he trotted across under the very noses of the horses. No hurry. In fact, he paused and rattled his collecting-box in front of the policeman, who felt obliged to dip his other hand into his pocket and drop in a coin. People all around laughed, and when Chance reached the pavement on the other side, he heard the chink of many more coins.

Outside the railway-station a bootblack cleaning the muddy boots of some City gentleman gave Chance a coin; so did his more prosperous-looking customer. A dozen hansoms with their drivers were waiting for fares, the heavily blinkered horses thrusting heads deep into nosebags; all the cabbies made their contributions. The collecting-box weighing so heavily that his back ached, he headed back to Chandos Street.

83

Loud triumphant barks announced his return and Dick Tozer quickly unstrapped the box. Chance, thankful to be free of it, shook himself vigorously and rolled round on the floor.

'What a weight,' Dick exclaimed, as he held the box up for Tom Woods and Jimmy Draper and the other firemen to see. 'Must be a quid or two here.'

They all patted Chance and scratched his back. The money was quickly added up. Mostly pennies, ha'-pennies, a few farthings from poorer people, threepenny bits and sixpences. Then shillings and florins glinted in the heap of coins. And a half-crown. And everyone shouted with joy. And another . . . And one more.

In all, Chance had collected £3. 18s. 7d. A lot of money in those days; and he was given an especially juicy bone as a reward for all that he had accomplished. One of the best bones he had ever enjoyed. With what Captain Shaw and the other firemen had contributed, the total sum amounted to nearly five pounds. The doctor who had owned Bob, and would have got five pounds for him from Jack Atchelor, also thought that the old horse had earned a better fate. He took the money, and so Bob would be given the proper burial he deserved.

THE BRAVE FIREMAN

With plunging steed the fireman comes along,
To fight the flaming foe.
He hears the shout of people as they throng,
And bid him onward go.
No danger he from fire doth fear,
Tho' the flames beat fierce and strong.
So the way we'll clear with a ringing cheer,
   As the fireman comes along.

    He gallops along, he gallops along,
    At the sound of the call ever ready,
      He gallops along with light heart and song.
   Then hurrah for the fireman steady.

No braver man than he in all the land,
When danger threatens nigh.
He's ever ready at the word's command,
Brave deeds to do or die.
By day or night some life to save,
To risk his own he dares,
For a fireman's heart is strong and brave,
He ne'er for danger cares.

    He gallops along, etc.
              ARTHUR ST IVES, *1909*

5. Watch-Dog of the Night

Man is a hunting animal. He delights in having
something to run after: whether it be a pickpocket
who has just eloped with watch or purse; a cat with
a can tied to its tail, a hare, a deer, a woman, a
fugitive hat. Something to chase, something to run
down, and ultimately destroy. But of all things to be
hunted, chased, run down, it's doubtful if there's
anything to equal a fire.   GEORGE AUGUSTUS SALA

London sleeps in peace because Captain Shaw and his
Fire Brigade are vigilant in the task of fighting the
fires that nightly threaten our city.   JACK WHILE

AFTER nightfall, when oil-lamps, candles and gas-jets
were used so extensively, and so many buildings left
unattended, when a spark, live cigarette-end or cinder
could get a hold unnoticed, this was the fireman's
busiest time.

In his office at headquarters Captain Shaw sat,
surrounded by telegraphic apparatus, his fingers on
the pulse of the metropolis, cognisant waking or sleeping of what was happening in every quarter, able
speedily to concentrate men and engines at any one
spot. He had divided London into four districts, three
north and one south of the River Thames. Every
station in each district was in telegraphic communication with each other, and with him.

On especially busy nights, when there could be
several fires to deal with in various parts of London,
he felt compelled to change his uniform two or three

87

times. Tons of water are hurled on to a fire, some of which is bound to drench the firemen. In his bedroom, neatly decorated in blue, he kept an array of uniforms, together with a row of thigh-high boots, all ready to hand at a moment's notice. Not that he was so partial to uniforms, he preferred the same casual jacket and trousers as worn by his men, when engaged in cleaning and maintenance work.

Born in County Cork, he entered Trinity College, Dublin, attained his M.A., had decided for the priesthood and was on the point of being ordained when 'At the very last moment, after even the ordination sermon had been preached, I retired furtively in my college robes, and leaving them in my college rooms took ship for America.' While in New York he nearly died in an hotel fire; returning to Ireland, he obtained an army commission, and then took over the reorganisation of the Belfast fire-force. He was aged thirty-one when he took on his present job following Braidwood's death.

He had a speaking-tube installed at his bedside, and whatever the hour, always had his wits about him. He once was awoken at 2 a.m. to be told that a fire had broken out in a back room over a coffee-shop in the Old Kent Road. 'One corpse burned to death.' Captain Shaw had the message repeated half-a-dozen times before the informant realised his mistake and corrected his report: 'One corpse burned.' What had really happened was that the fire had broken out in a room where a dead body was lying in a coffin.

Captain Shaw wrote various fire-fighting manuals, and travelled widely on the Continent, and in America, where his visits were not always conducive to better

The 'first' Chance, the dog after whom this story's hero was named. Painting by an unknown artist, about 1835

Wallace, Glasgow's fire-dog, complete with protective boots

Joe, of the City of Oxford Fire Brigade

Whitechapel's Bill; recipient, among other rewards, of the Royal Society medal

Chance. Painting, by an unknown artist, about 1883; probably destroyed in London Blitz

Tilling's greys. Impression of *Fire Queen*, Bruce and Betty on their way to a display before the Prince of Wales at Southwark headquarters

The Rescue: copies of this painting adorned every fire-station and fireman's home. It was duplicated, the helmet and jacket, altered to suit, by the New York Fire Brigade

Anglo-American relations; he was very proud of his own fire-fighting force, and didn't welcome criticism of their prowess by such as Fire Chief Cronin of Washington: 'American firemen are very superior to English.' At times considerable controversies raged to and fro across the Atlantic; but on the other hand, he and Chicago's Fire Chief Swenie hit it off, exchanging information useful to each other.

The Skipper ordered a type of long ladder he'd seen in use in America; and when in 1878 he had introduced the street-alarm to London, he experimented with the American Exchange Telegraph system, later changing it to a series-circuit invention by a man named Brown. It was these bright red, small, round boxes of the Brown's Buzzer Select Fire Alarms which were a feature of London's streets for the next fifty years. They worked on the single-wire system with an earth return and, though very reliable, were subject to faults that often resulted in false alarms being given. These, however, gave nothing like the trouble caused by the 'False Alarm Malicious,' usually started by mischievous children or drunken or irresponsible adults. At one time the nuisance was becoming so serious that Captain Shaw feared he might have to consider doing away with Brown's Buzzers, though he never did take this drastic action.

The telephone also arrived in London from America, almost simultaneously with the street fire-alarm, and, compared with the clumsy alphabetical telegraph system, greatly improved inter-station communication. But it was some years before the telephone began to be used by the public for calling the fire-brigade; the public street phone-box didn't appear until 1905, and private telephones were few, and, anyway, local post-offices did not at first consider the telephone a suitable medium for making alarm-calls.

Not only was he a personal friend of the Prince of Wales, but Captain Shaw was on good terms with Queen Victoria; she presented him with a fine clock which stood on his drawing-room mantelpiece. There was also a bronze statuette sculptured by Prince Victor of Hohenlohe-Langenburg (a son of Queen Victora's half-sister, Princess Feodora of Leiningen). The Queen herself had a copy of this statuette which is still kept in Windsor Castle.

Captain Shaw contrived to lead a busy social life; he was a member of the best clubs, quite the man-about-town, and was often the subject of cartoons in newspapers and popular magazines. Stories of his exploits and those of his firemen were recited or sung in the music-halls. A frequent first-nighter, he was at the first night of *Iolanthe* to hear himself depicted in Gilbert and Sullivan's opera, where the love-sick Fairy Queen sings:

> On fire that glows with heat intense
> I turned the hose of common sense
> And out it goes at small expense,
> We must maintain our fairy law.
> That is the main on which we draw
> In that we gain a Captain Shaw.
> Oh, Captain Shaw, oh, Captain Shaw,
> Type of true love kept under,
> Could thy brigade with cold cascade
> Quench my great love, I wonder?

Gilbert was accused of having borrowed the lyric from a music-hall song about that other heroic fireman:

> My heart's on fire,
> Not all the fire-brigade could
> Subdue the flames
> Though led by the Braidwood.

The Skipper was not permitted to dodge Fate's every blow; his personal courage and insistence on being in there with his men which earned him their respect, resulted in his being thrown from a ladder when Kesterton's carriage factory in Long Acre went up in flames one night. He suffered severe back-injuries.

As he was getting better, his wife received word that 'Her Royal Highness the Princess of Wales had graciously signified her desire to pay a visit of congratulation on her husband's recovery from the accident he had sustained.' The Royal party who visited Captain Shaw included the Prince of Wales, the Princesses Louise, Victoria and Maud, the Princess of Saxe-Meiningen, and the Grand Duchess of Mecklenburg-Schwerin. They drove to Southwark in three open carriages, and *The Times* reported that they were heartily cheered by the crowd as they passed through the gates.

In fact, the patient never really recovered from the effects of the accident. Years later he was to suffer the loss of both legs as an indirect result of his injuries.

Newspaper gossip-columns began to note that London's fire-chief often visited his fire-stations accompanied by a certain titled lady. In 1886 he was to find himself cited as co-respondent in the sensational

Campbell divorce-suit. Lord Campbell, son of the Duke of Argyll, suing Lady Campbell for divorce, named him together with the Marquess of Blandford and a General Butler. Lady Campbell cross-petitioned; citing Amelia Watson, housemaid in the Campbell home.

The confused case ended without a verdict for either side, but there was a good deal of bawdy gossip. Captain Shaw's involvement with this *cause célèbre* might easily have compelled him to offer his resignation. But as the magazine, *Society*, put it: 'He left the Court without a shadow on his fair name and his blameless, honourable and laborious life.' On the evening when the newspapers came out with the result, Captain Shaw went once again to a performance of *Iolanthe*. His appearance in the stalls was greeted with something like an ovation, a spontaneous demonstration of his continued popularity which he found very gratifying.

*

Three weeks after his meeting with the dancing bear, Chance saw him again. It was the night of the fire at the Philharmonic Theatre, Islington; and was an encounter which provided Jack While with as strange a story as ever he had reported.

He was on to it from the start. Captain Shaw had invited him to join him at Evan's Supper Rooms, on this very night. He had been to the famed eating-house a couple of times since he'd been obliged to forgo his father's invitation the night of the fire off Fleet Street, and enjoyed his visits. But tonight, all heads were turned on London's renowned fire-chief, and basking in the reflected glory made the occasion even more pleasurable for While. His eyes never failed to widen at the pyramids of dishes at the tables around him; the red-hot chops, sobbing hot tears of brown, frizzling fat, serene grilled kidneys, weltering proudly in their noble gravy. His mouth watered at the sight of a neighbour's Welsh Rarebit, streaming over and engulfing the toast like yellow lava; he sniffed the fragrant vapour of the corpulent sausage placed before the Skipper, He observed the russet hot potato first defy the knife, then yield through a lengthened gash to the melting influence of butter. And brimming pints of sparkling ale, or creaming Scotch, or brownest Burton; and hot whisky-and-water, mighty jorums of punch and grog; and the fragrance of potent cigars.

A sudden noise from the street. It grows louder, swells into a hoarse, jarring roar. The ballad-singer on the stage pauses in his song; conversation-buzz ceases; the waiters forget to rattle the change, a score of questions are raised. Then comes the mighty answer, echoed and re-echoed, and fraught with dread, the momentous word: Fire!

Above the noise from the street sounded a familiar, unmistakable barking. Captain Shaw was already making for the door, Jack While following, still wiping his chin with his table-napkin. 'I'd know that row anywhere,' the Skipper said. 'That dog, Chance, and my Chandos Street men . . .'

Where does a London crowd come from? Be the hour never so late, the street never so deserted, a cry of 'Fire' would be sufficient to attract a mob, growing

93

instantly thicker and noisier. Whether they start from the sewers or the cellar-gratings, or drop from the chimney-pots or the roof-copings, they gather some-how, to jostle, squeeze, yell. Now, they gaped as *Fire Queen* swung off from the Strand, up through Bedford Street, into the narrow streets of Long Acre, Covent Garden and High Holborn, on towards Islington, Chance well ahead, as usual, clearing the way.

'Coach' nursed Bruce and Betty up the incline from Theobalds Road, then put them full-pelt when the street ran downwards to gather impetus to take *Fire Queen* up the next gradient; and Chance, backed up by the 'Hi-ya-hi's', warned everyone to keep out of the way.

The previous night, the manager of Islington's Philharmonic Theatre had invited Captain Shaw, who had been on a routine fire-precautions inspection, and for whom like all theatre-managers he had the greatest admiration, to see the performance. The orchestra had even played the National Anthem as much a compli-ment to him as in honour of the Queen. He had bowed and smiled at the applause, little realising how soon he would be back.

Now, tonight, after the theatre had emptied, it caught fire. By the time *Fire Queen* reached the scene, adjoining houses were alight, and the area blacked out by billowing clouds of smoke. Jack While encountered Dick Tozer, seated for a momentary respite, on a rolled-up hose, mopping his blackened face with a handkerchief. 'I'm sure,' he groaned, 'to get the sack tomorrow.' He explained how a few minutes earlier he had taken a hose into the theatre basement in an attempt to reach the heart of the fire. Glancing back he had seen through the smoke a figure standing at the basement entrance, doing nothing. Dick shouted out to him with impatience, using some expressive epithets, to help him ease the hose into the cellar. The figure at the basement-entrance made no move, and Dick's choice of language flowed freely. 'All right, Tozer,' the figure finally said, and rapped out an order to another fireman to help Dick. 'I could have fallen flat on my face,' Dick told While, 'when I heard the Skipper's voice.'

While reassured him. 'Captain Shaw's too much of a gentleman himself to notice you were using a bit of ungentlemanly language – so long as you were on the job.'

By the early hours the fire was under control.

Fire Queen was heading away, and was passing a house next door to the theatre, or what was left of it, when Chance let out a bark, and disappeared down a side-street. Dick Tozer, 'Coach', Jimmy Draper and the rest wanted to go home: it was still dark, there was an acrid smell of smoke and burning, and the stench of steam arising from the gaunt ruins around them. Dick made out Chance ahead and saw his shadowy figure pause by a gate. He jumped down and hurried after him.

Even as he reached the gate, Chance barked and jumped up in an attempt to push it open. He thudded against it, his claws scratching noisily as he endeavoured to tear a way in. There was something inside he wanted to get at. 'What is it? What's the matter?' Dick asked him.

For answer, Chance whined and barked. He jumped up at him, clicked his teeth in that horrid way he had, and in no uncertain manner told Dick that the object of his interest lay beyond the gate. The occupants of the house had been driven out by the smoke which still hung around the building, and had obviously not returned. Dick put an arm over the top of the gate, pulled back a bolt, and pushed it open. Chance rushed past, through the door of a stable, barking and making a terrible commotion. Windows overlooking the yard opened, heads appeared, abuse was shouted down.

Chance's barking suddenly stopped and he appeared in the stable doorway, whining and glancing back. What was it then, that had attracted his attention? Dick swung his lamp so that its beams pierced the smoke-filled interior and fell upon a huge, dark shape huddled in the corner. For a moment he couldn't make it out. Chance ran forward, sniffed and whined and turned back to him agitatedly. Dick realised that it was a bear. Its tight muzzle had been removed, but it was tethered by the chain attached to its steel collar to a ring in the wall. The glazed eyes were open and it lay obviously suffocated by the smoke. It was dead. Its owner had rushed away in alarm and had not bothered about the bear.

Chance sniffed round its head, and his tail drooping, came back to Dick with a piteous expression. Two or three times he returned to sniff at the dead bear, and in the end went out, whining, tail between his legs. Dick followed, very much upset by the sight of the bear that had been left to die on his own, forsaken.

Jack While got on to the story, and confirmed that

it was in fact the dancing bear that Chance had encountered the day he was collecting money for old Bob, when he had behaved as if he had wanted to prevent the bear being taken off. Had he known that it was to Islington, and the stable where it was to die? Could Chance have foreseen what was going to happen?

The bear was removed and buried; its owner never returned to claim it. But Dick never forgot the sight of that huge dark, furry shape in the darkness of the stable. Chained to the wall, suffocated to death.

And the strange way that Chance had known it was there, and had tried to save the bear, but had been too late.

ODE TO A LENGTH OF OLD HOSE

Worn and cast, done for at last,
Thy day is gone, thy time has passed;
Condemned Hose, thy die is cast.
For forty years thou has been tried
By sturdy firemen, side by side,
Seeking out the post of danger.
To sturdy hands thou art no stranger,
While rushing through thee a saving stream
Destroyed the fearful red fire's gleam;
Thou erst wert strong, no leakage there,
Thou would'st any amount of pressure bear;
But, like old men with port-wine gout,
Tho' sound to look at, thou'st worn quite out.
And, as to Hose we cannot give a pension,
Thy virtues here have 'honourable mention.'
And, dear old friend, oft as we met together,
At drills, or fires, you never shew'd white feather.

M., *1st March 1881*

6. A Nose for Danger

Towards ten o'clock in the morning screaming swarms
of sea-birds darkened the sky above the town of
Concepción on the Pacific Coast of Chile. At 11.30 the
dogs fled out of the house. Ten minutes later an earth-
quake destroyed the town.

ADMIRAL ROBERT FITZROY, *1835*

Very slight tremors . . . affected the dogs so much
that for several moments their whining was heard
all over the town. VITUS B. DROSCHER,
The Magic of the Senses

THAT autumn, one of London's frequent fogs started
up, a real pea-souper. Yellow and ebony clouds rolling
up from the river surged among the shipping and lay
in the rigging and along the docks. In great swirls of
black and yellow it came up from the Essex Marshes.
The new factories all around London belched forth
smoke on the still, cold air; flakes of soot fell like
dirty snow upon the streets.

Chance spent most hours of the day and night at
Chandos Street. Although alarm-calls continued to be
received, fire-engines had difficulty in finding their
way to a fire, and Dick Tozer kept a sharp eye on
Chance because there was always the risk of him being
stolen. He in turn kept close to Dick. In those days,

dog stealing flourished. Even Queen Victoria's King Charles spaniel, Cherry, was stolen.

A detective-sergeant named Kendillon, of C Division, was given the job of trying to recover the Queen's pet, and as a result of information received, learned that a notorious dog-thief, Teddy the Fish, was the culprit. He had kept Cherry in a Seven Dials' thieves' den, and was about to sell it to a confederate for £50 when Sergeant Kendillon caught up with him.

Cherry was returned to Queen Victoria, who appointed a Select committee in the House of Commons to inquire into dog-stealing crimes. Sporting editors, dog fanciers, ships' captains, the police, and even known thieves, gave evidence before the Committee. The Editor of *Bell's Life*, well-known for his contacts not only with dog-owners, but with those who stole them, exposed a gang who made a living out of the business; prices paid for stolen dogs ranged from £10, £20, £50, even up to £150 for a spaniel. A certain steamer-captain plying between London and Rotterdam took as many as twenty dogs at a time, usually on a Sunday, in one voyage. The Commissioner of Police, Sir Richard Mayne, learned that over the past three years, 157 dogs were known to have been stolen, while 1,688 were 'lost', to be returned to their owners at a price. Chance had become so well-known, if a thief got his hands on him he would be worth a good ransom, up to £100 Dick Tozer reckoned, and the other firemen agreed.

The fog had barely cleared when early that evening the alarm clanged, Betty and Bruce were swiftly in their places, and *Fire Queen* was away. It was a warehouse off Lower Thames Street. Tom Woods noticed that Chance was no longer rushing ahead, barking to clear the way, instead he kept alongside Betty, staring up at her anxiously, and giving short barks of encouragement. 'Faster, Betty,' he seemed to be telling her. 'Faster . . . Faster . . .' 'Coach' realised that Betty wasn't, in fact, pulling her weight; that young Bruce beside her was doing much more of the work. He joined in with Chance. 'Giddy-up . . . Giddy-up . . . Get a move on, Betty . . . Get a move on . . .'

Immediately he felt her response. Her ears flattened, her head came up on her arched neck. But there was something wrong. She wasn't her old self and he suddenly remembered how before the thought had flashed across his mind that there was something amiss with her. Then the thought had gone. Now, there seemed no question about it. As he shouted and urged her he frowned to himself. Out of his long experience he knew that a horse is usually very well or very ill. A horse is either up or down. Fighting fit or at death's door. Nothing in between.

Now *Fire Queen* was being slowed down by the throng hurrying to the fire. Great sheets of flame were roaring up round the warehouse roof, fanned by the wind that gusted off the river. As Dick Tozer and his comrades went to work there came a loud cry. 'A fire-boat – there's a fire-boat coming.' Sure enough, chugging up at full speed was the London Fire Brigade fire-boat. Speedily, it came up alongside, her hoses cascading powerful streams of water into the blazing warehouse.

'Coach' led Bruce and Betty off down the street to

where they could wait in safety. He saw Chance fussing round Betty, which was an odd thing for him to do. He usually made a bee-line for the fire, enthusiastically dragging out pieces of burning wood, or whatever he could find in an effort to help. But now, his anxiety was all for Betty. Tom Woods saw her limp. It was her left foreleg. She stopped, almost guiltily, as if she was afraid he had seen her. Chance had glanced up at her. Did he realise that Betty was trying to hide the fact that she had gone lame?

A sudden cry came from a knot of people staring down at the river. A woman was calling out that a boy had fallen in. Chance made as if to dart forward, paused and gave a look at Betty. Then his shiny eyes fixed on 'Coach'. Again, the cry, and Chance spun round and shot off.

Into the crowd on the river-bank he charged, clearing a way. He came to a halt, his toes grasping the very edge, to peer down at a small boy struggling in the water, his face piteously white in the flare of the flames. While watching the blaze, he had stepped backwards into the river. 'He'll drown,' the woman screamed, and others added their voices to hers. 'He'll drown – Help, someone, he'll drown . . .'

Chance, tongue lolling out, tail wagging furiously, poised on the brink for a split second, let out a bark and dived in. As the boy rose to the surface, gasping for breath, Chance reached him, got his jacket-collar in his teeth. The crowd shouted encouragement, while the flames from the burning warehouse lit up the scene.

One of the crew of the fire-boat jumped into a skiff and rowed swiftly to help. Quickly he hauled the boy

Look-out on roof of Southwark headquarters, from which a fire's location could be observed and communicated to Captain Shaw by speaking-tube

Night duty at a street escape-station and watch-box

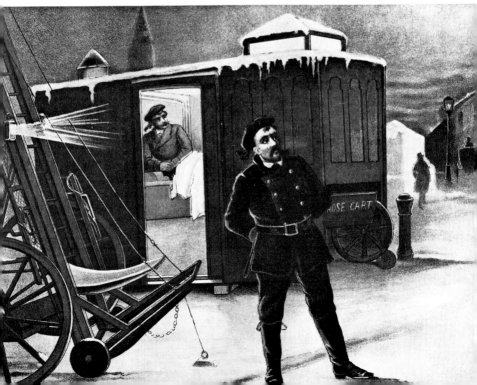

Captain Eyre Massey Shaw, 'the Skipper'

The Prince and Princess of Wales awarding medals at a review of the London Fire Brigade in Hyde Park

The silver helmet and kit of Fireman No. 116 – the Prince of Wales – was kept in readiness for him at Chandos Street

Saved From The Flames

aboard, lugged Chance in, and both were safely put ashore.

Someone wrapped some sacking round the boy, who was sobbing with mingled fright and thankfulness at being alive. Chance shook himself briskly, which quickly scattered everyone round who'd started to pat him, and ran back to the blaze.

Could he read human beings' thoughts? Or were his so-called telepathic gifts due simply to extraordinary sharp powers of observation? Chance couldn't recognise anyone at a distance; he would rely on his sense of smell to give him that information. But at close quarters by studying Dick Tozer's movements, the tone of his voice when certain events were about to take place, Chance learned to relate the action or tone in the voice to what happened next.

This was how he learned the trick of escaping from a falling wall of a blazing building. It was by running towards it. From observing Dick he learned that it was a matter of watching the wall. The windows of a burning building are the first to be destroyed, leaving empty spaces in the walls. He saw how he stood far more hope of escaping injury by moving into the space as the wall fell than if he'd tried to run away – a wall is certain to collapse more quickly than he could run and would overtake him. Accordingly, as soon as Chance saw a wall falling towards him he made for the gap left by the window.

He could, for that matter, get through smoke faster than any fireman, and was much quicker in finding anybody injured, lying in the fire. Now he could clamber up a fire-escape even before Dick Tozer, upon whom he could rely to carry him down again (that was the difficult part); he could break in a window with the hind part of his body and enter backwards. A method which he had learned for himself.

He had learned, too, that the crowd's excitement at a fire might unnerve a fireman, when, for instance, descending a ladder with a rescued child or a woman. A sudden cheer could imperil the fireman; or seeing him up an escape trying to effect an entrance, women in the crowd might shout all kind of alarms, which could distract him and endanger his life.

The firemen were getting the blaze under control, when Chance darted off in the direction of Bruce and Betty. He reached them and immediately started barking. 'Coach' holding both horses' bridles, wondered what had got into him; he was barking more loudly, as if urging Betty and Bruce to move away. He began jumping up at Tom Woods, who felt impelled to shift Bruce and Betty.

At the moment that he stepped forward, he heard a curious crumbling noise. He looked up and gave a shout. The wall under which Bruce and Betty stood was collapsing. Even as he yelled, he dashed forward and dragged Bruce and Betty barely inches clear as the wall collapsed in a thick cloud of dust and rumble of bricks. Chance had also leapt clear.

What had happened was that the fire had crept insidiously along from the warehouse, behind the wall, and this was what Chance must have heard. A dog can hear noises that very often a human being can't.

Coughing as the dust from the falling wall tickled his throat, 'Coach' led Bruce and Betty along the street to *Fire Queen*, muttering to himself how truly wonderful Chance was. 'If it hadn't been for your warning,' fondling his head, 'we'd have been goners.' Chance's shiny eyes stared up at him, and he wagged his tail in acknowledgement of 'Coach's' gratitude.

He trotted off to where Captain Shaw was giving a fireman named Sprague a helping hand directing a jet of water into some smouldering embers. There was a sudden crash of bricks, and he looked up at the warehouse wall with an anxious eye. Chance gave a warning bark. 'Carry on,' the Skipper said. Sprague threw another look upwards. 'I'll tell you when to run for it.' Sprague kept the hose going. Captain Shaw watched him. Chance barked several times. The warehouse wall didn't collapse, however, until three days later.

Weary, their faces blackened, their uniforms scorched, Dick Tozer, Jimmy Draper and their comrades were thankful that the night's work was over as *Fire Queen* moved off; behind them the warehouse, black and gaunt, smouldered in the early light as the night began to fade in the sky. As the begrimed, saturated crew, stomachs empty, weary to exhaustion, passed some workmen on their way to start their daily round, one of them shouted: 'Good old firemen, that's right, go home and have a good rest and sleep,' never realising that the firemen were, in fact, going back on duty, ready at an instant's notice to answer another call.

As he returned to Chandos Street, 'Coach' experienced the same hunch that he had felt before that all was not well with Betty. But he couldn't make up his mind what was amiss. Later as he watered and fed her and Bruce, and was giving her a shrewd look, he suddenly realised that Chance wasn't anywhere to be seen. He asked Dick Tozer and Jimmy Draper if they'd seen him. They were finishing a good meal; Dick, who had thought Chance was with Bruce and Betty, hurried into the street. The grey light of dawn was creeping over the rooftops. He heard the hoot of a ship's siren down river. Another day was beginning. But there was no sign of Chance.

'Are you sure he's nowhere about?' he said to Tom Woods.

'Coach, shook his head. 'And you know him,' he said. 'You'd know if he was around all right. He'd be barking and jumping about.'

Dick looked worried. Had Chance been stolen by some dog-thief?

Where was he?

*

He was, as a matter of fact, outside the house of Mr Youatt, noted veterinary surgeon, in Newman Street, off Oxford Street. Every few seconds Chance raised his head in the direction of the bedroom window and gave a bark. Mr Youatt was shaving, during which he hated being disturbed. It made him jump so that he was afraid of cutting himself. He carefully put down his cut-throat, as his razor was called and, drying his chin, opened the window.

'Oh, it's you.' He knew Chance. He was one of several veterinary surgeons employed on contract to look after Tilling's horses wherever they were stabled, including fire-stations, their job to keep a horse sound in his feet and free from ailments.

Knowing how intelligent Chance was, Mr Youatt realised that he hadn't called at that early hour just to chat about the weather. He had obviously brought some important message. Making quite sure that he hadn't put his razor down carelessly, so that it might slip and cut a piece out of the bedroom carpet, Mr Youatt popped downstairs and let Chance in.

At Chandos Street Fire Station, when Tom Woods went to groom Betty and Bruce, the first thing that riveted his attention was Betty's foreleg. It was her left one. The way she was standing. The moment he saw it, he knew what the trouble was. Betty at once tried to stand normally, but it was too late. She couldn't disguise from him this time that she was lame.

He gave her grey neck an understanding, affectionate pat. 'All right, Betty, let's have a look.' With a firm, gentle hand, he encouraged her to lift up her hoof. He knew at once that this was a job for Mr Youatt. He let Betty put her foot down, this time very carefully to the ground. Her ears twitched. She seemed to understand that he was sympathising with her. He turned to go out of the stable; he would have to send for Mr Youatt right away.

'Hello "Coach",' came from the doorway.

'Mr Youatt – you're just the man I was thinking of.'

'I thought you might be. Isn't that why Chance was on my doorstep first thing this morning?'

'Coach' looked past him and there was Chance, wagging his tail with a knowing look in his shiny, dark eyes. Mr Youatt explained how Chance had turned up at his house to impart, quite obviously, that he was wanted urgently at Chandos Street. He had given Chance a drink of water and a biscuit, and together they had come along to the fire-station.

Mr Youatt was examining Betty's foreleg and, right away spotted the trouble. 'A navicular condition.'

'Coach' might have had difficulty spelling the word, but he knew very well that Betty was suffering from pain in a small bone in her foreleg. It was at the pivot where the tendons came up from the hoof to just below the fetlock. The trouble was due to London's hard road surfaces and cobbled streets, which continually jarred the horses' legs as they galloped over them. Betty's lameness was permanent, Mr Youatt said gravely.

As they went out of the stable Tom Woods shook his head sadly. He knew how upset Betty would be when her days as a fire-horse were done. Peaceful retirement at the Catford home for horses wouldn't be the same as life at the fire-station. Was that why she had deliberately tried to hide her lameness? 'Coach' agreed with Mr Youatt that it was better for her to retire now; if it was left too late, the pain would become unbearable and she would have to be destroyed.

Dick Tozer and the other firemen looked in to give Betty a sympathetic pat and a piece of sugar to cheer her up. She continued to pretend that she hadn't gone lame, although you would have thought that she must have realised from the unusual attention being paid to her that she hadn't deceived anyone. Anyway, she put a brave front on it and behaved as if she was still going to remain in her job. Bruce gave her sympathetic nudges every now and again, as if to tell her that everything would come out right for her in the end.

Arrangements were made for her to be replaced by a new horse. A message went to Mr Goodwin at Thomas Tilling's, Peckham.

It was then that Chance took himself off again. Where had he got to this time?

FIREMAN ASHFORD

(Killed in the execution of his duty at the
burning of the Alhambra Theatre.)

Give kindly thought to those who fought
That great Alhambra fire;
Poor Ashford, dead, has laurels won
To which Kings would aspire.
Up ladder high, on roof too weak,
Such acts as his, like heroes' deeds
Will never cease to speak.
A fire that like a furnace roars,
And flames do upward leap.
Hark! What was that din?
A shout! A crash!
The roof has fallen in!

Now will the Firemen cease the fight?
Or, dauntless courage prove?
Yes, still they face the dreadful roar
Nor backwards do they move!
Tho' a whirlwind rushes round them,
They at their post remain,
Mid the hissing, mid the roaring,
Mid the hurricane of flame!
Each carries out his orders
From The Skipper all revere,
Full well they know, to him each man
Is a comrade dear.

(Give kindly thought)

Give kindly thought to those who fought
That great Alhambra fire;
From duty, none would shirk it,
From danger, none would fly —
But like poor Ashford, or the rest,
Be wounded, crushed, or die.
Then honour to our Firemen,
His comrades of that night,
And honour to our noble Prince
Who sadly leads the van
Of each one's grief and sympathy
For Ashford, brave fireman!

R. J. DAWSON, 1st January 1883

7. His Last Alarm

'Tis sweet to hear the watch-dog's honest bark
By deep-mouth'd welcome as we draw near home;
'Tis sweet to know there is an eye will mark
Our coming, and look brighter when we come.

BYRON

It has even happened to me to be warned by the
behaviour of a dog of the approach of death. What
does he know about death? At least as much as we do,
probably a good deal more.   AXEL MUNTHE

MR GOODWIN had that day attended the horse sale
at the Elephant and Castle Repository, where the
chief auctioneer, a man named Alfred Harris, resplen-
dent in black top-hat, stood on his rostrum, hammer
aloft. 'Ten guineas? Only ten guineas for this high-
class gentleman's hunter. Why, he would kill for
fifteen. May I say eleven? Ten-and-a-half, then? Run
him in again, Jack,' this to one of the grooms, who ran
the horse down the repository, scattering the onlookers,
while Mr Harris continued, 'There you are, gents,
worth twice the money.' The horse returned to face
him, nostrils quivering and knees trembling slightly,
while the groom scratched his cane along the cobbles
to make the old nag prick up its ears and look its
best.

Not the sort of horse Mr Goodwin was looking for,
so over the river to a horse sale at Aldridge's Horse
Repository, at the top of St Martin's Lane, in those

days well-known for its saddlers' shops, like George Baker & Sons; Parker & Parker; Thomas Parker & Company; and Schombergs.

But nothing appealed to Mr Goodwin on this particular occasion, and he was about to leave to return to Peckham when who should run up to him, barking as if he were an old friend, but Chance. He couldn't understand what it was all about, but Chance quickly made it clear that he intended to stick to him. Even when he got into his pony-trap to drive to Peckham, Chance barking and wagging his tail, his eyes as bright as ever, jumped up and sat determinedly beside Mr Goodwin, who gave a shrug and drove off.

Presently, arrived at Thomas Tilling's, Chance jumped down and trotted round the bus-station, greeting the horses he knew, and the drivers coming and going with their buses, wheels rattling, harnesses jingling. He even managed to enjoy a nice bone which a kind bus-conductor gave him.

Soon he was making friends with Poppy, who had done over four years' service with the buses and was a strong, young horse. Chance fussed about her, just as he'd done with Bruce on that previous occasion, and Poppy whinnied at him in a friendly way.

Meanwhile, Mr Goodwin received a message from Chandos Street: a new horse to replace Betty. Returning to the stables, and no sign of Chance, Mr Goodwin decided that he was probably on his way back to Chandos Street.

It was late that night, in fact, when Chance did turn up, and Dick Tozer and 'Coach', Jimmy Draper and the other firemen were thankful to see him again.

Though he wasn't able to go into any details about where he'd been this time, he reciprocated their welcome with a bark, tail wagging nineteen to the dozen. It had been a long day for him. This was the second journey he'd made within a few hours, and Peckham's a goodish distance from Chandos Street. Very soon he was curling up in the stable where Bruce stood alone, an empty place next to him, on his face an expression which could best be described as one of self-satisfaction.

Awake next morning early, he was rushing into the street and back into the fire-station again. 'Acting just the same as he did before Bruce arrived,' Dick Tozer said to Tom Woods. Just after breakfast, he grew even more excited. Eyes popping, he was off into the street and back, barking and causing a great commotion.

And, sure enough, here was Mr Goodwin with a beautiful grey.

'This is Poppy . . .' he started to say, only to be interrupted by Chance, who was jumping up at the new horse, as if welcoming an old friend. 'I'll tell you something about that dog,' Mr Goodwin said, when he could make himself heard. 'Do you know where he was yesterday afternoon? Up at Tilling's, he was, making friends with her.' 'Coach' and Dick Tozer looked at Poppy, then at each other and nodded. The same thing as had happened over Bruce. 'It's as if he knew that she was meant to come here,' Mr Goodwin continued. Chance was almost turning somersaults in his excitement. Poppy whinnied and shook her beautiful, grey mane, obviously equally glad to be at her new home. 'Look at them, just like old pals meeting up again.'

'Coach' nodded and led Poppy to the stable where Bruce was standing. Chance followed him, and Mr Goodwin pushed back his billycock hat and scratched his head. 'Beats me,' he said to Dick, 'how could he have known it was Poppy who was going to replace Betty?'

'He's a strange dog,' Dick agreed. 'Got second sight, I shouldn't wonder.'

When Mr Goodwin finally left, he was still muttering to himself that when it came to the matter of a dog, he would rather have a horse every time. Knew where you were with a horse, you did.

Chance didn't forget Betty. He used to go with Dick Tozer, or some of the other firemen, out Catford way, to see her at the horses' home. He would bark and jump up at her, just like old times.

Poppy quickly settled down, 'Coach' putting her through her paces, well-satisfied with her; and two nights after her arrival she was racing alongside Bruce with *Fire Queen* to the Alhambra Theatre, Leicester Square, which was on fire. Chance was out ahead, of course, and dashing back to Poppy, keeping an eye on her.

*

The Alhambra Theatre, famous for its music-hall entertainment, opera, ballet and all sorts of musical shows, was almost completely destroyed that Thursday morning, the 7th of December 1882. A few minutes before 1 a.m., a detective named Bowden, returning off-duty to Police Section House nearby, saw smoke pouring out of the theatre dress-circle windows, and promptly alarmed Chandos Street. By the time *Fire Queen* was there, huge volumes of smoke and columns of flame swept up from the burning building. It was like daylight. *Fire Queen* had been quickly followed by fire-engines from King Street and Southwark, which played upon the building front and back, but still the flames belched forth, still the smoke hung overhead in a dense cloud, relieved by myriads of brilliant sparks.

Half-an-hour after the fire had started the roof fell in with a loud crash, a gigantic column of forked flames pierced the mass of smoke and lit up the sky with startling effect. Although the roof had gone, the two towers flanking the building, north and south, stayed intact. Even when the fire had nearly burnt itself out, and Leicester Square and Soho had again lapsed into comparative darkness, these two towers were still licked by circling wreaths of flame which shone out like beacons from the smoky murk.

So swift, so complete the catastrophe, nothing was saved; furniture and fittings, wigs and properties of the actors and actresses all shared the same fate. Under the direction of Captain Shaw, steady streams of water were poured on to the burning theatre from *Fire Queen* and other engines stationed in Castle Street, Bear Street and Green Street. But the fire raged with fierce intensity. The central flagstaff fell from the roof into the roadway beneath, snapping in two like a match-stick. Firemen managing the escapes from which they directed the hoses, were warned by Chance, barking his head off, just before the flagstaff fell. They got out of the way in time.

It wasn't until half-past three that morning that the firemen gradually gained mastery over the fire in the worst part, the northern wing of the theatre which faces Leicester Square. In the centre of the theatre, and also in the southern wing the fire still burned. Beyond the blackened masses of masonry flames still leaped, while the crash of falling timber could be heard.

Aided by the torrents of water still being poured on the building by the firemen, the fire by four o'clock that morning showed signs of being under control. The theatre was gutted from roof to floor, only the skeletal masonry stood. All that remained of the splendid interior with its lavish appointments were charred rafters.

Jack While, quickly on the scene to report the sensational story, noted the curious coincidence that the name of the production being rehearsed at the time was *King Comet; Or Love of the Flame and Icicle*, its ten thousand pounds' worth of costumes destroyed. Even by Thursday afternoon, Captain Shaw knew that a large incandescent mass still glowed beneath the blackened crust of charred beams and wreckage, and firemen continued pouring streams of water into the middle of this area. The auditorium, built in the form of a Byzantine amphitheatre now had a desolate appearance, Saracenic arches against the bare scorched walls added to its strange, barbaric look; and there was an equally strange entanglement of girders.

Jack While had hurried round to the stage-door entrance and stood chatting with a fireman named Ashford, from Watling Street Fire Station, together with Dick Tozer and Jimmy Draper. Chance came up barking excitedly, to be followed by the Skipper and the Prince of Wales, in his fireman's uniform looking begrimed and scorched as any of them. He produced his big cigar-case. 'Well, Shaw,' he said, handing it round, 'I think we've all earned one.'

Jack While took a cigar, thanking the Prince, then decided he would keep it as a souvenir. But as he tried surreptitiously to wrap it in a page torn from his note-book, Chance jumped up at him, barking furiously.

'What are you doing?' the Prince asked, seeing what was occurring. Embarrassed, the reporter explained that he would like to have kept it as a souvenir of the occasion – he didn't add that he felt he could have given Chance a sharp kick for not minding his own business.

'Very well,' was the reply. 'But have another to smoke now.' Jack While lit up the second cigar; and he grinned down at Chance, who had done him a favour, after all; the Prince had a fine taste in cigars, and now he had one to smoke and one to keep as a memento to treasure.

An hour later, Jack While learned that it was the last cigar Ashford ever enjoyed; he was killed by a falling wall.

Three nights following the Alhambra Theatre holocaust, *Fire Queen* was called to some large printing works off the Gray's Inn Road, which were ablaze, and next to them an empty private house. The fireman named Sprague was in the basement of the house, directing a hose on to some flames, when there was an explosion of gas, and the house fell in like a pack of cards.

Chance was caught by part of a collapsing wall, and yelped in agony, but nevertheless went straight to where Sprague lay buried and scrabbled away at the debris in an effort to get at him. Dick Tozer and Jimmy Draper, helped by police and bystanders, with Chance limping, but doing his share, at length managed to remove the bricks and rubble from Sprague's head. He was still alive, and stimulants were passed to him. John Burns, M.P., who was a great friend of the firemen, was on the scene, and took Sprague to Charing Cross Hospital, where he died four hours later.

First thing next morning Dick Tozer carried Chance in his arms to Mr Youatt in Newman Street. Although characteristically he had tried not to show it, he had been badly injured when the wall hit him. Mr Youatt at once diagnosed internal injuries. He thought it best for Chance to remain in his care, and he remained with Mr Youatt for three weeks. But he got no better, there was nothing to be gained by keeping him where he was; he was pining for his friends at Chandos Street, and finally Dick carried him back to the fire-station.

He was made as comfortable as possible in a corner of the watch-room in a basket, tucked up in a blanket, looking very wretched and nursed in turn by Dick, or Jimmy Draper, or 'Coach', or any of the other firemen. Next day the Prince of Wales, accompanied by Captain Shaw, came in and did his best to cheer up the patient. The station wasn't the same place. No Chance rushing about, jumping up at everyone, barking and clicking his teeth. He just lay there, his once-shiny eyes dull and half closed, without any apparent interest in what was going on.

The next night the alarm went. Suddenly Chance's head came up and his eyes shone. Dick Tozer, who was with him made to hurry for his jacket and helmet. With a bark that ended in a painful yelp, Chance jumped out of the basket. Dick turned as if to take him with him. Even as he held out his arms, Chance went rigid, gave an odd little whine and fell back beside the basket.

He lay still as death.

Dick shouted to the fireman left on watch-room duty to take care of Chance until he came back, although he knew that there was nothing that could be done for him. At dawn *Fire Queen* returned; Dick, 'Coach', and the others crowded round Chance. He hadn't moved since the firemen had rushed off.

Outside the pink in the sky was just beginning to gleam greenish-blue in the east. The firemen, aching with weariness, were about to get themselves some food and drink, when the alarm clanged. Another fire, and they must race off to it. Dick Tozer, tears marking his begrimed face, hadn't left Chance. Now, he leapt up, and as he did so heard a yelp. He stared back, disbelievingly. *Chance had struggled to his feet.*

The alarm had called him back from death itself. He swayed for a moment, his glazed eyes raised on Dick Tozer. He gave another feeble bark. Then he collapsed. It was all over.

He was still there in his basket when Dick and the others once more returned. He hadn't moved. This time, he was dead.

Dick, 'Coach', Jimmy Draper and the other firemen

subscribed a sovereign each to have the body stuffed and mounted. The job was given to a regular professor at the art of taxidermy, and Chance was placed in a handsome case, plate glass front, three feet six inches long by two feet two inches wide, with an enamelled and gilt border. Above, on a scroll, was inscribed the date of his death and:

'Stop me not, but onward let me jog,
For I am Chance, the London fireman's dog.'

Below this the names of the Chandos Street firemen, headed by Dick Tozer, Jimmy Draper and Tom Woods.

Chandos Street didn't get back Chance in his case for some time. The cause of the delay was discovered quite by accident. What had happened was that he had been borrowed in all his gilt and glass splendour by a customer of the taxidermist who exhibited him in a fair in the East End of London. Crowds were flocking to see him, paying a penny a head.

It was Jack While who heard about this and told Dick Tozer. In ordinary clothes and paying his penny, Dick went along to see the show.

It was Chance, all right. Prudently, Dick said nothing and went off, to return soon afterwards with Jimmy Draper and several others from Chandos Street. They demanded and obtained Chance in his glass case.

He stood on a table at the back of the watch-room. But only for a short while. Even in death he had an opportunity to serve.

Sprague's widow and three young children had been left destitute, and something had to be done to raise money for them. It was Dick Tozer, enthusiastically supported by Jack While, struck with the drama and human-interest of the story, who suggested that Chance, complete in his splendid case, should be raffled. It was precisely the sort of thing that would have appealed to him; had he been asked he would have replied with loud barks of agreement. Not only every fire-station in London entered the raffle – it was sixpence for a ticket – but everyone in the neighbourhood of Charing Cross who had known and loved Chance, bought a ticket.

Such was his fame that the raffle raised the sum of £123. 10s. 9d. Though who actually won him was, oddly enough, never discovered. Even Jack While failed to find out the winner's name. What, then, finally happened to Chance? Glass case and all, he just vanished from sight. Never seen again. Or was he?

*

Captain Sir Eyre Massey Shaw – he had been made a C.B. in 1879 and was knighted in 1891 – retired on the 31st of October 1891. During his thirty years as London's fire-chief his men dealt with 55,004 fires, averaging over five per day, 86,645 'chimney calls', and 32,335 false alarms. He went to live at Folkstone, but was to be seen, despite the loss of his legs, in a bath-chair at the great annual social occasion, the Church Parade in Hyde Park, where, every year, he would be greeted by his many friends.

He died at Folkstone on the 25th August 1908; newspapers and journals at home and abroad devoting many columns of space to his fine achievements. At his funeral his old friend and fellow-fireman, the Prince, now King Edward VII, was represented by Sir Archibald Elphinstone; crowds thronged the route to Highgate Cemetery, where he was laid to rest in Fireman's Corner.

By then the fire-station at Chandos Street had been transferred, *Fire Queen*, Dick Tozer, 'Coach', and the rest, to Scotland Yard, not very far distant from Chandos Street. Chance would have found his way there easily, and on the night of Captain Shaw's death, Dick swore that he could hear the howling of a dog running up and down outside. He and another fireman went out and both were positive that they saw a dog who resembled Chance jumping up – the other fireman even heard him click his teeth in that shuddersome way that set his own teeth on edge.

Chance's ghost?

It depends upon whether you believe in such things, human beings' ghosts, or the ghost of a dog?

After all, it isn't as if he was any ordinary dog.

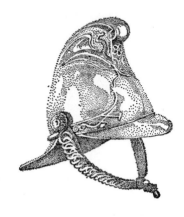

IN MEMORIAM OF A FIREMAN

So, the tired hands are folded,
    Still the true heart in his breast,
And the busy brain is quiet
    In its long and dreamless rest;
And the watchful eyes that ever,
    O'er the loved one kept their guard,
Under nerveless lids are sightless;
    Gone to heaven for reward.

Never more with welcome warmth,
    Shall that kind face press our own;
Hushed the sweetest strains of music,
    That our ears have ever known;
Faded out the tender love-light,
    With its warm and steady glow,
That was never dim or waning,
    Never flickering or low.

Over him will spring the roses;
    Over him the violets bloom;
Over him the fragrant lily
    Shed its delicate perfume.
All that earth has fair will gather
    In remembrance of our dead;
After-types of all the beauty
    He upon our lives has shed.

Anon, 1st September 1881